News Search, Blogs and Feeds

CHANDOS
INFORMATION PROFESSIONAL SERIES

Series Editor: Ruth Rikowski
(email: Rikowskigr@aol.com)

Chandos' new series of books are aimed at the busy information professional. They have been specially commissioned to provide the reader with an authoritative view of current thinking. They are designed to provide easy-to-read and (most importantly) practical coverage of topics that are of interest to librarians and other information professionals. If you would like a full listing of current and forthcoming titles, please visit our web site www.chandospublishing.com or email info@chandospublishing.com or telephone +44 (0) 1223 891358.

New authors: we are always pleased to receive ideas for new titles; if you would like to write a book for Chandos, please contact Dr Glyn Jones on email gjones@chandospublishing.com or telephone number +44 (0) 1993 848726.

Bulk orders: some organisations buy a number of copies of our books. If you are interested in doing this, we would be pleased to discuss a discount. Please email info@chandospublishing.com or telephone +44 (0) 1223 891358.

News Search, Blogs and Feeds

A toolkit

LARS VÅGE
AND
LARS ISELID

Chandos Publishing

Oxford · Cambridge · New Delhi

Chandos Publishing
TBAC Business Centre
Avenue 4
Station Lane
Witney
Oxford OX28 4BN
UK
Tel: +44 (0) 1993 848726
Email: info@chandospublishing.com
www.chandospublishing.com

Chandos Publishing is an imprint of Woodhead Publishing Limited

Woodhead Publishing Limited
Abington Hall
Granta Park
Great Abington
Cambridge CB21 6AH
UK
www.woodheadpublishing.com

First published in 2010

ISBN:
978 1 84334 602 9

British Library Cataloguing-in-Publication Data.
A catalogue record for this book is available from the British Library.

Typeset by Domex e-Data Pvt. Ltd.

Contents

List of figures

All illustrations are copyright of the owners of the source applications and websites. Every effort has been made to obtain the copyright owners' permission to reproduce them. Any errors or omissions should be notified to the publisher for rectification in future printings.

List of abbreviations

ABC	American Broadcasting Company/Australian Broadcasting Corporation
ABN	Asia Business News
AFP	Agence France-Presse
AP	Associated Press
API	application programming interface
ARD	Arbeitsgemeinschaft der öffentlich-rechtlichen Rundfunkanstalten der Bundesrepublik Deutschland
BBC	British Broadcasting Corporation
CBC	Canadian Broadcasting Corporation
CBS	Columbia Broadcasting System
CCTV	China Central Television
CNN	Cable News Network
DDP	Deutscher Depeschen Dienst
DN	*Dagens Nyheter*
DPA	Deutsche Presse-Agentur
HTML	HyperText Markup Language
ICON	International Coalition of Newspapers
IDW	Informationsdienst Wissenschaft

IPS	Inter Press Service
ISIN	International Securities Identification Number
ITAR-TASS	Information Telegraph Agency of Russia
JCN	Japan Corporate News
KWIC	keyword in context
MeSH	Medical Subject Headings
MSNBC	a name combination of Microsoft and NBC
NAICS	North American Industry Classification System
NBC	National Broadcasting Company
NER	named entity recognition
NHK	Nippon Hōsō Kyōkai (Japan Broadcasting Corporation)
NLP	natural language processing
NMS	news monitoring service
NPR	National Public Radio
OPML	Outline Processor Markup Language
PBS	Public Broadcasting Service
RSS	really simple syndication/rich site summary
SACSIS	South African Civil Society Information Service
SDI	selective dissemination of information
SNST	social networking services and tools
UPI	United Press International
URL	uniform resource locator (for example, web address)
XML	Extensible Markup Language
ZDF	Zweites Deutsches Fernsehen

Acknowledgements

We would like to thank our families for their continuous support during the writing of this book – without their patience it might never have been completed. We also thank our editor, Jonathan Davis, for his patience, for giving us helpful advice when needed and for showing his trust in us by extending the deadline for this project. We dedicate this book to our fathers, who have both passed away during the last few years. We miss you very much.

About the authors

Lars Våge is an academic librarian at the Mid Sweden University Library in Sundsvall in the north of Sweden. He grew up in Gothenburg, where he attended the university, studying such diverse subjects as pedagogy and Greek. He has been an information professional for nearly twenty years, working in various areas of librarianship. He currently is a systems librarian and also teaches information retrieval to students in the Information Technology department. His special interest is internet search and blogs and he has written several books and articles on these topics in Swedish. The book *Informationssökning på Internet*, co-authored with Lars Iselid and Hercules Dalianis, is commonly used as a textbook in Swedish universities. He is also the co-author of the first book in Swedish on the blogging phenomenon, *Bloggtider*, published in 2005. In 2006 he published a report for the Swedish Institute of Democracy (DEMICOM) concerning blogs, internet censorship and freedom of speech. He has lectured on and given courses on internet searching, news search, blogs and the semantic web in numerous cities in Sweden. Lars has twice been a speaker at the Gothenburg Book Fair. He has also spoken about European search engines at the Online Information Conference in 2007 in London. In collaboration with Lars Iselid he has maintained a Swedish blog reporting on internet search engines since 2001. He has three sons and spends most of his free time with his family when he is not jogging or listening to (what they call) incomprehensible music.

Lars Iselid is an Information Architect at the Swedish IT company Teknikhuset, where he is working with digital library solutions. He grew up in Skellefteå, but moved to Umeå to study diverse subjects such as art history and ethnology at the university. After graduating as a librarian at the University of Borås in 1993 he worked for 16 years at Umeå University Library – 2 years in the Loan department, 12 years in the Medical Library and 2 years in the Digital Library department. He has written books, book chapters and many articles for computer magazines and library journals. In collaboration with Lars Våge he has maintained a Swedish blog reporting on internet search engines since 2001. Also since 2001, he has frequently been a speaker in Sweden, Norway and Finland. He was elected Information Specialist of the Year in Sweden in 2010. He has two daughters and a son and his greatest interests beside his family are soccer, computers, running, reading and writing.

Preface

This is a book about searching for news. More specifically, it's a book about searching for news online. This can be interpreted in two ways. First, it can be understood to mean searching for news that's been published online, and second, it can also mean searching for news, printed or otherwise, using an online search interface. This book is about both. Mostly it's about using free news search tools on the web, but it's also about using professional online services and news monitoring services. However, its scope isn't limited to searching for news articles. Many interesting stories and comments on stories are published today in blogs, and so we also cover the blogosphere and how you can search for blog posts and discover new blogs with interesting content. Newer additions to the media landscape, such as podcasts and social media, are also investigated in a news-related context.

Chapter 1 discusses the nature of news search and what we can expect to find using the news search tools. An increasing number of people now use the internet as their first stop for finding news, and news search engines can be instrumental in providing them with a much wider range of stories than ever before.

In the second chapter we concern ourselves mainly with free news search tools. Here we give an account of how free news search engines have evolved from the mid 1990s onwards. The tragic events that unfolded during September 2001 became the catalyst that gave rise to the rapid development of new and powerful tools for searching news online. Major players in the search engine field realized the necessity of robust, specialized news search engines that could cover a significant proportion of the articles and stories with news value that were published around the world on the web. In this chapter we describe in detail the most popular and useful of the currently available free news search services. The diverse mix of news sources that appear in their results lists are also explored. Google News and other news search engines index not only newspaper sites but also, to a varying degree, broadcast news, news agency material, press release wires and many more specialized information sources. Although these search engines mainly cover news published on the web, some also offer limited search possibilities for printed news. A section on the numerous historical newspaper digitizing projects is also included towards the end of the chapter.

Chapter 3 is devoted to the fee-based online news services that are available to those willing to pay for news search. Many companies, organizations and even individuals have very urgent information needs that cannot be satisfied with the free tools. In this chapter we describe the many advanced searching facilities that the professional news services offer to their users. The power of the manual indexing that enables much more precise searching is also considered. The main emphasis is on features that can be found within the so-called 'Big Three', namely Factiva, Dialog and LexisNexis. Their amazing scope and coverage empower the users of these services to find almost anything that has been published in the printed versions of many of the major news publications. However, we must remember that, for legal reasons, they cannot provide the full text of articles written by freelance journalists. This means that sometimes the conscientious searcher may have to resort to slowly browsing through the pages of publications using a microfilm reader.

In Chapter 4 we take a look at the various news or media monitoring services that offer convenient business intelligence to stressed professionals. These services provide an easy way out of your informational dilemmas, but can be rather costly to subscribe to. The quality and scope of their monitoring vary considerably and a thorough analysis of what you need and whether they can satisfy your demands is essential. Some of the free news search engines offer keyword-based search monitoring in the form of email alerts and RSS feeds. The professional search services described in Chapter 3 can also be used for monitoring. They are very good at this and will possibly enable you to fine-tune your searches in many more ways than do some of the dedicated monitoring services.

In Chapter 5 we pause to discuss how you can evaluate different news search tools. It can frequently be difficult for users to compare them and make the right choices, and so we have tried to outline key components of a well-functioning news search environment. Some suggestions for manual evaluation procedures are also presented in this chapter. What is most important for individual users will of course vary, but it is hoped that some general remarks will be of value to most people interested in these questions. If we don't pay attention to and react to inconsistencies and complain to the search companies, their services will perhaps not evolve in the way they should.

The explosive growth of blogs during the last decade has changed the web forever, and many interesting stories are now being written by bloggers all over the world. The initially hostile reaction to the blogging phenomenon by professional journalists has given way to a more relaxed relationship and many of the most active and influential bloggers today have a background in the media world. Chapter 6 is about the blogosphere and how to search in blogs and discover new blogs to read. After trying to define what a blog is we attempt to trace both the history of blogs and the evolution of blog search engines. This is followed by an inventory of the most powerful blog search tools that are currently at our disposal, such as Google Blog Search, Bloglines, Technorati, BlogPulse, IceRocket and a few others. Also several large blog directories are mentioned that can be browsed to find blogs on almost any topic.

If you don't know what RSS feeds are, or have just heard these words, Chapter 7 is for you. The extraordinary power and versatility of the simple XML format generally referred to as Really Simple Syndication has opened up many interesting possibilities. This is especially true for those with an interest in news-related content. This is because many newspaper and other media sites today publish their material in RSS versions as a complement to the normal web versions. What's particularly good about RSS is that you can subscribe to these feeds within so-called 'feed readers' that can effectively automate a lot of your web browsing for you. RSS is also frequently used to enable monitoring of keyword searches in news and blog search engines, and even in research databases. We describe in detail some of the best RSS readers, such as Google Reader, Bloglines and Netvibes. There is also a section on podcasts, an interesting new development that relies on RSS to deliver video and audio content.

Currently a lot of the buzz on the internet is focused around what are called social media or social networking services and tools. A prime example of this trend is the emergence of microblog services such as Twitter. In Chapter 8 we look into this new media scene in relation to news search. Many prominent people, bloggers and even journalists now have their own Twitter streams that are followed by their colleagues, friends and fans. As in normal blogs, the twitterers often include links to news stories within their posts. It has become increasingly important to be visible in social media networks, and tools for searching and monitoring this new sphere have evolved rapidly.

In Chapter 9 we present some concluding remarks, chosen to highlight some of the key points from the preceding chapters. They are presented in the form of advice and recommendations and are not intended to be a full summary of the book. We have also included a list of abbreviations and list of recommended further reading.

We cannot guarantee that the user interfaces of the search engines described in this book will appear in the same way when you, the reader, try them out. News search engines change their appearance and features quite frequently and there is always a risk that what one writes will become outdated in some way. But we like to try, anyway.

Introduction: the nature of news search

Abstract: News search on the internet began to develop only following the events of 11 September 2001 in the US. The online audience for news is continually growing; even so, a large amount of news content is still available only in print media. Content can range from news articles, press releases, photos and news agency output to blog posts, video and podcasts. There are differences between what newspapers publish in their print and web editions, and not everything can be found using the free news search engines; further, the text of articles by freelance journalists can often still be accessible only via microfilm. The free news search engines, commercial databases, professional search services and news monitoring services all provide different coverage, levels of indexing and search facilities.

Key words: news search engines, news sources, web news.

This introduction explores the nature of news search and its relationship to different news sources such as newspaper websites, news agencies, broadcast news, press release wires and blogs. Although news search engines started to appear in the mid 1990s it became painfully obvious in 2001 that there was a very real need for powerful news search tools on the internet. This started the rapid development by major search engine companies of specialized news search engines to crawl and index major news sources in near real-time. Even though a vast quantity of news articles are constantly being published on the web, there is still a great deal of content that is available only in the printed versions. News search engines also face many difficulties resulting from the unstructured nature of web news as compared to the more structured and more easily indexed printed articles.

Discovering the power of news search

> Although many use the terms 'news' and 'journalism' interchangeably, I think that journalism also encompasses something much more important – context. (Matt Thompson, Reynolds Journalism Institute, University of Missouri)[1]

One of the first examples of the power and significance of news search on the internet occurred in the autumn of 2001; more specifically, on 11 September, when two hijacked airliners destroyed the World Trade Center in New York. Servers at several western media sites broke down because of the numbers of people desperately seeking for news on the internet about the traumatic event. Google reported that search for news-related content increased by a factor of 60 on that date.[2] That morning a message on the Google front page said: 'If you're looking for news, you will find the most current information on TV and radio.' In the afternoon Google showed only direct links to media sites and cached copies, and again the message to use TV and radio (Figure 1.1).

In those early days, when Google was not yet so dominant, it didn't have a specialized search engine for news. Search engines overall were not such powerful tools for finding current news as they are nowadays, and not

Figure 1.1	In the afternoon of 11 September 2001 Google's home page linked to news sites, including cached copies as they appeared earlier

Breaking news: Attacks hit US

Many online news services are not available because of high demand.
Below are links to news sites, including cached copies as they appeared earlier.

Current: Washington Post - Yahoo! News - CNN - ABC News - Yahoo! News Photos - NY Times

Earlier: CNN.com - NY Times (1) - NY Times (2) - Washington Post

many put any extra effort into crawling news sources more frequently than other sites. The autumn of 2001 was a milestone in the transition not just of traditional broadcasting media such as radio and TV, but also of the internet and search engines as tools for finding and navigating information about current events. In July 2003 Krishna Bharat, who conceived the idea for Google News, wrote in *Google Friends Newsletter* that: 'Following September 11, I realized it would be useful to see news reporting from multiple sources on a given topic assembled in one place.'[3] This was actually written a long time after the first appearance of news search, although it was still in a state of immaturity.

News searching and browsing is currently one of the most popular activities on the internet. According to a survey conducted by Pew Internet and published in August 2008, 70 per cent of all American internet users are online on a typical day. Thirty per cent of them check news and 49 per cent search online. This activity was surpassed only by email, which 60 per cent of Americans used.[4] Pew Internet also did some surveys concerning the 2008 presidential campaign and found that 6 out of 10 internet users went online in 2008 for campaign news.[5]

Pew discovered that many news consumers are turning to alternative distribution channels and different 'screens', even for news coming from traditional media sources. Among those who had read a news story from a newspaper organization on the previous day:

- 69 per cent had read a printed copy of a newspaper
- 61 per cent of those who used the internet (representing 52 per cent of all news readers) had read a news story online on a computer
- 6 per cent of cell phone owners had read a news story on a cell phone, and 7 per cent had done so using a Blackberry, iPhone or some other Smartphone.[6]

The online newspaper audience is constantly growing. Statistics from the Newspaper Association of America show that in the US it was 42 per cent of the total internet audience in April 2009, up from 26 per cent in December 2004. In December 2004 each visitor looked at 36 pages and spent 34 minutes reading. By April 2009 this had increased to 46 pages per visitor and 40 minutes of reading.[7] Searching and browsing news is not just an important activity for everyday users; it's also extremely important for many professionals doing business intelligence tracking, both of their competitors and of their own brand.

The concept of news and its relations

Let us explain what we mean by the term 'news'. News is seen as an official message about something important that readers didn't know about before: an event, a process or some kind of condition. News reporting, in turn, is about how mass media, for example newspapers, collect and prepare news. 'Mass media' refers to those channels of communication that are designed to be consumed by large audiences, primarily newspapers, TV, radio and the internet. We could also include films, magazines and books; on the internet we could point to videos, blogs and podcasts. Also, we shouldn't forget the web accessed via mobile phones and game consoles.

News can be presented in many different media, as we have just described, and a news publisher can use many different channels. Using only the printed newspaper format provides an opportunity to write text and show pictures; using radio enables the use of audio; while television can use moving pictures, audio and written text. The internet and mobile phones provide the possibility of using written text, showing pictures and videos and also playing audio such as online radio or podcasts. In that respect the internet and mobile phones present news publishers with an opportunity for a significantly richer media experience, but this also means bigger challenges – especially when it comes to generating revenue from the free provision of news.

Today many different kinds of news and news-related content are published, such as news articles, press releases, stories from news agencies and blog posts. The results pages of many news search engines contain a confusing mix of all these different kinds of written content. In some cases videos, news photos and podcasts are also included in the results.

A press release (PR) is commonly described as a written or recorded communication sent out to the news media from an organization, a public institution or a company for the purpose of making the receiver aware of something with news value. It is often sent by regular mail, email or fax; and many use commercial newswire services to distribute their press releases. Press releases are not written objectively, but rather with the aim of marketing a product or promoting a statement. In some cases PR marketing agencies are hired to write them, which means there can be a degree of divergence between the originator and the writer, even when the release is approved by the originator. Many journalists read press releases and write their own news stories based on them. It is hoped that these will be more objective, but often they merely confirm what has already been stated in the press release.

Newswires from news agencies are used both by newspapers themselves and by news search engines. When there is a news drought it's not uncommon for some issues of local newspapers to be completely dominated by stories from news agencies, with very few stories produced by newspaper staff. A news agency can be commercial, with the purpose of selling news, like Reuters and UPI; others work in cooperation with media companies and distribute their news centrally, like Associated Press (AP) and Agence France-Presse (AFP). There are also a lot of non-profit news agencies. The South African Civil Society Information Service (SACSIS) focuses on social justice news and analysis of policy dialogue in South Africa. Indymedia focuses on political and social issues. Zenit reports on the Catholic Church. There are also government-controlled news agencies like ITAR-TASS in Russia and Xinhua in China.

To gain more insight into the possible biases or hidden agendas of some types of news agencies you have to check the organizations and financing behind them. SACSIS is governed by a board of trustees drawn from civil society, such as activists and practitioners working in academia and non-governmental organizations (NGOs). Indymedia is run by, as it puts it itself, 'a collective of independent media organizations and hundreds of journalists offering grassroots, non-corporate coverage' and has its origin in the anti-globalization movement. Zenit is run by the non-profit organization Innovative Media, with donors initially from

Catholic Church organizations. Some of the most influential news agencies overall are AP, UPI, Reuters and AFP.

Blog posts are, in some respects, a news-related product of this decade. There is a big debate concerning the decline of the traditional printed newspaper and the emergence of social media sites. Newspapers have completely failed to get paid for content (other than financial information, such as in *Wall Street Journal*), and some people think that the paid content model is effectively useless.[8] Newspaper after newspaper has cut its workforce during the last few years. For example, the US circulation of paid weekday newspapers during the six months ending 31 March 2009 fell by 7 per cent to 34.4 million, as compared with the same period the year before, according to figures released by the Audit Bureau of Circulations.[9] This may not seem much, but the decline has been a constant for several years. At the same time online newspaper traffic has increased,[10] as have online advertising revenues. The American writer and teacher Clay Shirky has written a long blog post about this, and here is one short statement upon which to reflect:

> Society doesn't need newspapers. What we need is journalism.[11]

You could change the word 'newspapers' to 'record companies', and 'journalism' to 'music'. Or why not 'publishers' and 'stories'? The internet has given journalists, musicians and writers an opportunity to break the power of the newspaper editor, the record label owner and the book publisher.

But the purpose of this book is not to delve deeply into the debate concerning the decline of traditional newspapers, so let's stop here. Despite the changes that will come, news will still be hard currency, and because more and more are going digital, news will be even more hard currency in connection to search, monitoring, discovery, browsing, aggregation and much more. Maybe during the coming decade we'll see journalism's bigger migration into other channels than the traditional newspaper.

So what impact will social media and citizen journalism have on this change? A lot has been written about this during the last few years, and certainly social media are here to stay in some way or form. To take the example of blogs, a lot of people still look on them as just diaries on the internet. However, many news media organizations have recruited both their own journalists and celebrities to blog on their sites. Blogs are often a mix between a column and a diary; and everyone who regularly reads several blogs knows that they have more dimensions to them than just the diary aspect. Many bloggers write about new things happening, such as new products, new technology, new research being published. It's not very different from what you can read in traditional newspapers, but there's a different kind of expression, sometimes lacking the reflection of journalists. It's generally more subjective; sometimes it's ranting, with no editor-in-chief monitoring you. As a blogger, you build your own brand.

Today we know that a lot of interesting news is written and discussions of news topics take place in blogs and forums outside the traditional media sites. Allowing comments on news stories is more or less a given if you want to take your online readers seriously. Comments first started as a technical functionality in blogs, and it took a long time for the major newspapers to accept that the traditional input in the printed editions, consisting of letters to the editor, has largely moved to the comment fields. With comments we have the ethical dilemma of readers being able to rant anonymously. In printed newspapers there are anonymous letters to the editor, but most editorial offices at least require you to submit your name and address before you can be published anonymously. However, there is still an unending debate as to whether or not readers should be permitted to comment anonymously in blogs.

News published on the web vs printed news

It's important to understand that there's often a big difference between what newspapers publish on the internet and what's published in the printed edition. This was perhaps more obvious 10 years ago, but with the adoption of the internet as the first stop to check for news we tend to forget it. This is why it's important when searching for news to distinguish between news that's published on the web and what's in the printed editions. Most free news search engines index only those news stories published on the web. Google has done some indexing of older printed news articles (the earliest articles indexed by Google News Search have publication dates before 1840), but not of any current material. For this reason printed news articles, especially their full text, have to be searched and retrieved from commercial news databases. However, the commercial news databases don't include freelance stories, can be selective in their indexing of some sources and may omit very short articles.

A telling example of this occurred in Sweden in 2008.[12] *Dagens Nyheter* (DN) is one of Sweden's biggest daily newspapers and Presstext is a commercial news database that has indexed its articles from 1992 onwards. Mikael Löfgren, a Swedish freelance journalist who has written many articles for *DN* about the global justice movement, discovered that a researcher had missed important articles about the global justice movement in his doctoral thesis. Why was this? The student, Magnus Wennerhag, had searched Presstext using his keywords and claimed that he had found all the articles, a total of 335 items, published in the five biggest Swedish newspapers in which the global justice movement had been mentioned during the years 1999–2006. The problem was that Presstext doesn't index articles by freelance writers in *DN*, which meant that Wennerhag had missed all the articles written on this subject by Löfgren.

The only way to find all printed newspaper articles is to go to a library that holds microfilm of the original printed issues. But there is no guarantee that it will have a database index of all the articles for the period in which you're interested. For instance, there is no publicly available bibliographical database in Sweden that has indexed all the articles from *DN* for the time period in which the above-mentioned Wennerhag was interested. In fact Löfgren stated that only the employees of *DN* had access to such an index. Therefore you often need to know exactly what you want and when and where it was published; otherwise your only option is to load the microfilm and manually browse your way through the newspaper issues – a very time-consuming task. At the very least national libraries should keep an archive all the newspapers published within a country and have a significant number available on microfilm. Public libraries in some larger cities and academic libraries will also have some newspapers on microfilm.

Structured vs unstructured news content

Before news articles began to be published on the web, news search was traditionally performed in bibliographic databases. The advantage of this was more structured data with precise information on authors, titles, sources and publication dates. It was only with the emergence of blogs that the first example of a more structured format than HTML appeared on the web. This format was RSS, which is an XML application that can be used to mark up blogs and other content with metadata. News sites soon began to publish their content using RSS as well. Thanks to the wide use of RSS in blogs and on news sites it has become easier to build news search engines because of the structured metadata that can now be extracted. However, many news sites publish only headlines and lead paragraphs from their articles in the RSS versions.

The different types of news search tools

In this book we have tried to make a distinction between three types of news search tools and have devoted a chapter to each. The three categories are:

- free news search engines
- commercial news search databases
- news monitoring services.

Of course this is not a perfect categorization because some news search tools can include elements from two or even all three of these categories.

The first category, free news search engines, is probably the one of which the general public are most aware and which they may occasionally use. This group includes the news search engines of the major search contenders like Google, Yahoo! and Microsoft. We call them 'free' because the search engines are free to use and the news material they index is, in most cases, available for free on the internet. It's important to remember that the content indexed by them is only news published on the web in HTML and/or RSS formats. The exception here is Google News, which indexes older printed content, accessible via a special News Archive Search. It should also be pointed out that some of the search services that in other respects fit the description of the second category, i.e. commercial news search databases, will let you search their databases for free, while the full text of articles must be paid for.

Commercial news search databases emerged long before the internet, when other online research databases like ERIC, Medline and Compendex were established in the late 1960s and early 1970s. In the commercial news databases you will frequently find nearly all of what is published in the printed editions. The exception in this case is articles written by freelance writers, as discussed above. Professional search services such as Factiva, LexisNexis and Dialog have a full set of advanced search features that enable you to construct very complex and precise search queries. If you don't find the full text within these databases you can contact your local library, which will help you to search the library databases to find a library that has access to the full text in some form. The library will also help you to order photocopies if it doesn't have what you need in its own collections. This can be a very slow process if you're used to getting the full text of news articles with just a few mouse clicks using a general web search engine.

Finally, we have the news monitoring services that automatically scan news articles from a list of important sources. They typically deliver search results using email or, in some cases, RSS. Using these services, clients can create their own search queries and get regular updates without having to repeatedly perform manual searches on different sites or in various search engines. News monitoring services often use both free news sources and sources that they pay a fee to be able to scan. For this reason many of these services can be quite costly – but then again, there is a huge market in selling news monitoring services to individuals, corporations and organizations that have a need for business intelligence. The free news monitoring services usually scan only news published on the web. There are also some news and blog search engines that offer free monitoring services. Using Google News, for instance, you can create search queries and have the results delivered by email or as RSS feeds. Many of the professional search services also offer monitoring services for their paying customers.

Notes

1. Matt Thompson, 'Newsless?' Newsless.org, 3 September 2008, www.newsless.org/2008/09/hello-world/.
2. Richard W. Wiggins, 'The effects of September 11 on the leading search engine', *First Monday*, Vol. 6, No. 10, 1 October 2001, http://firstmonday.org/htbin/cgiwrap/bin/ojs/index.php/fm/article/view/890/799.
3. Google.com, 'Q&A with Krishna Bharat of Google News', *Google Friends Newsletter*, July 2003, p. 2, www.google.com/googlefriends/morejul03.html#qa.
4. Pew Internet & American Life Project, 'Almost half of all internet users now use search engines on a typical day', Pewinternet.org, 6 August 2008, www.pewinternet.org/~/media/Files/Reports/2008/PIP_Search_Aug08.pdf.pdf.
5. Pew Internet & American Life Project, 'The online political news audience has grown dramatically over the past two presidential election cycles', Pewinternet.org, The Internet's Role in Campaign 2008, www.pewinternet.org/Reports/2009/6--The-Internets-Role-in-Campaign-2008/3--The-Internet-as-a-Source-of-Political-News/2--Online-news-audience.aspx?r=1.

6.   Pew Internet & American Life Project, 'Significant numbers now read newspapers and watch newscasts on their computer or mobile device', Pewinternet.org, The Internet's Role in Campaign 2008, www.pewinternet.org/Reports/2009/6--The-Internets-Role-in-Campaign-2008/3--The-Internet-as-a-Source-of-Political-News/4--Mobile-news.aspx?r=1.

7.   Newspaper Association of America, *Newspaper Websites*, www.naa.org/TrendsandNumbers/Newspaper-Websites.aspx.

8.   Arianna Huffington, 'The paywall is history', Guardian. co.uk, 11 May 2009, www.guardian.co.uk/commentisfree/2009/may/11/ newspapers-web-media-pay-wall.

9.   Robert MacMillan, 'US newspaper decline worsens', Reuters.com, 27 April 2009, www.reuters.com/article/rbss Publishing/idUSN2741442820090427.

10.   Brian Solis, 'Growth for newspapers online? Yes and no', Briansolis.com, 28 January 2009, www.briansolis.com/2009/01/growth-for-newspapers-online-yes-and-no.html.

11.   Clay Shirky, 'Newspapers and thinking the unthinkable', Shirky.com, 13 March 2009, www.shirky.com/weblog/2009/03/newspapers-and-thinking-the-unthinkable/.

12.   Mikael Löfgren, 'Faktafiltret: Mikael Löfgren om Bonniers, upphovsrätten och forskningen', Aftonbladet.se, 11 June 2008, www.aftonbladet.se/kultur/huvudartikel/article2661785.ab.

2

Free news search

Abstract: The first free news search engines appeared in the mid 1990s. Among today's more important news search engines, Yahoo! began developing its news website in 1996. Google News, Topix and Bing News have all made their appearance since 11 September 2001. This chapter highlights the free news search tools available on the internet today. The major free search engines offer advanced search features, a range of display and presentation options and clustering of stories from different sources. Free news searching is also available from a range of news sources, among them the major newspapers and their archives, news broadcasters, news agencies, and press and scientific newswires. Historical material is accessible through newspaper digitization projects.

Key words: news search, news search engines, news sources.

Introduction

It's now nearly 15 years since the first freely available news search engines appeared on the web. This chapter starts by tracing the history and development of these news search tools. Several of the currently available free news search engines enable you to search a variety of news sources offering free content. The majority of these sources make their stories available for only a limited time, while some others have a longer back archive on the web. There are also news databases and search services that will let you search for free but charge for viewing the full text. In a sense, these are free news search engines too. In this chapter we describe some of the most important tools currently available, such as Google News, Yahoo! News, Topix and Bing News. We also look at the different types of news-related sources, including newspapers with web archives, broadcast news, news agencies, press release wires and newspaper digitization projects.

A short history of free news search

The first free news search tools appeared on the internet in 1996 (Figure 2.1). Already in June 1995, InfoSeek had started providing a service called a personal newspaper for its subscribers. At that time you had to pay to use InfoSeek, which was then a combined web directory and database of articles from computer science periodicals. However, its Net Search, which was a search engine indexing the web pages that its crawler program found on the internet, was free of charge. Its News Search was a part of the services that were later offered for free and became an early favourite among the free news search services.

The personal newswires that InfoSeek introduced in 1995 were created by allowing users to automatically run search queries at certain intervals on indexes consisting of web pages, Usenet newsgroup messages and commercial sources. The later free InfoSeek News Search searched the contents of news wires from news agencies such as Reuters and press release wires like Business Wire and PR Newswire. In addition, you could also search national news sources on the web, such as USA Today, CNN and ABC News. InfoSeek

Figure 2.1 InfoSeek offered several types of news search in 1996

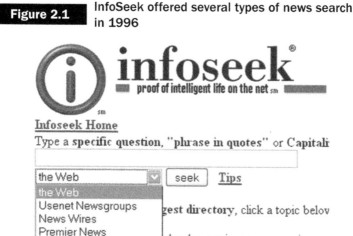

was acquired by Disney in 1999 and was subsequently terminated in 2001.

In 1996 at least two interesting news search sites were launched that didn't belong to any major company: Newsindex.com, in April, and Totalnews.com, in October. Newsindex.com boldly described the motivation for providing its service as a mission to let users find the truth. It argued that no single media outlet could do that, and that only by being able to access several sources could the reader get behind the headlines and find out what was really happening. It also stated that it wanted to do more than merely search the wires and the big media outlets and added many other websites with quality news content to its service.

Newsindex.com provided a current awareness tool as well as a facility to search its database directly. However, searching was limited to stories that were up to a maximum of one week old. Totalnews.com, on the other hand, provided an archive that sometimes enabled you to retrieve articles that were as much as a year old. *The Times* (of London) accused Newsindex.com of copyright infringement – something that would be repeated many times in the future with other news search engines and other news companies and organizations. In some countries news search engines have been very controversial and have come under attack from writers' organizations and copyright holders, while in others it is felt that the news search engines drive traffic to the source sites, and this is seen as being very good for the source sites with the original content.

The most popular website for searching the web at this time was Yahoo! and it continued to be so for many years. Starting from 1996, it added several other services to complement its immensely popular web directory. Its Yahoo! Daily News section initially offered content mainly from Reuters. During succeeding years it added more sources, including wires like AP, Business Wire and PR Newswire, and also some news websites. In 1998 it began to include content from international wires like AFP and Deutsche Presse-Agentur (DPA). It remained a limited wire-oriented search engine, but this changed when, through a chain of company acquisitions, Yahoo! gained possession of the powerful Norwegian search engine AlltheWeb, created by FAST Search & Transfer.

Another popular early search engine was Excite, which was created by students at Stanford University, just as Yahoo! had been. The burrito-loving youths who started Excite launched their NewsTracker in February 1997 (Figure 2.2), in their press release calling it the first free news clipping service on the web. They initially indexed sources such as the *New York Times*, *Fortune*, *Sports Illustrated* and other news media sites. News wires were added later to NewsTracker and it was possible to search both types of sources simultaneously, even if the results were displayed separately. Excite didn't manage to survive the turbulent years and, like InfoSeek, it was sold and its search technology abandoned in

Figure 2.2   Excite NewsTracker was launched in 1997

News**Tracker**

Finding it harder to stay on top of the news?
Just specify your topics and let NewsTracker do all the work for you

2001. The Excite@Home portal, however, continued to exist with changed content.

Many users came to embrace the newer Northern Light search engine, launched in 1997. This was AltaVista's (see below) main competitor, in having the largest web search engine index at that time, and introduced many new advanced search features. It created a set of specialized search engines called Special Editions that were much appreciated, and the concept was a novelty at the time. Its Current News Search was one such topical search engine, and became available in September 1998. It claimed that its index of news articles was updated every 15 minutes. It covered news wires only, but a broad selection of these could be searched simultaneously. Northern Light was bought by a company called Divine, which subsequently went bankrupt, and it disappeared from the free web in 2003. Northern Light Current News Search was one of the few news search engines available in September 2001.

One of the most important news search companies to emerge during the late 1990s was San Francisco-based Moreover. It provided a free news search engine and later also started licensing its database to companies like AltaVista and Inktomi. The latter delivered search technology for Microsoft's MSN portal and had its own search engine, available at HotBot. The HotBot News Channel didn't index wires, but only a selection of the most popular news media sites, and it was known for having the most current index of this kind of news content. In March 2001 Moreover became the supplier of news search for AltaVista. Because of this AltaVista was the most heavily used news search engine in September 2001 (Figure 2.3), while the leading search engine, Google, had nothing to offer in this way. Moreover has continued to provide news search for many major clients and today offers a broad selection of topical RSS news feeds for free.

One of the very best English-language news search engines outside of the US was **Rocketnews**, based in Ottawa, Canada. Although it became available late in 2000 it was formally launched in October 2001, shortly after the terrorist attacks in the US. Rocketnews became known early on for its excellent news search, and most particularly for having a very up-to-date index. In fact it offered a search engine for articles that were five days old at the most. It introduced a free RSS reader in March 2004, later the same year became one of the first to support search results delivered as RSS feeds, and shortly after that started offering blog search as well. It also added another feature – tracking your previous

Figure 2.3	AltaVista offering access to news search and news sources after the 11 September 2001 attacks

News Search:

terrorist attack   [Search]

Aftermath of the Attacks

AltaVista News, ABC, BBC, Boston Globe, CBS, CNN, CNN en Español, MSNBC, New York Times, Time Magazine,
USA Today, Washington Post

Disaster resources:

New York Times emergency list, Survivor-list sites

searches and building on these to enhance search results. In this busy year it became the first to offer a news search API and the following year, in 2005, it introduced its powerful desktop news search tool. In 2006 it expanded its search to audio and video news, and even podcasts.

In the aftermath of the events of September 2001, both Google and its main competitor in the fight for the world's largest index of web pages, AlltheWeb, started thinking about creating their own news search. AlltheWeb launched its news search engine in November 2001, whereas the first beta version of Google News didn't appear until the year after. The AlltheWeb news search engine was extremely powerful and almost immediately became the most comprehensive one available. Unfortunately, it was little known outside of Europe, and Scandinavia in particular. AlltheWeb had access to extremely fast reindexing technology and this became apparent in its news search. It also indexed much more non-English-language content than any of the other news search engines and offered many powerful search features.

In 2003 AlltheWeb gave up struggling to compete with Google and sold its web search division to Overture. This was a controversial company that provided sponsored search listings to many big clients around the world. It was for this reason that it, in turn, was soon bought by Yahoo!, which wanted to create revenues from this thriving new part of the search world. The news search technology created by FAST for AlltheWeb News was inherited by Yahoo! and became an integral part of **Yahoo! News**. At this time Microsoft had not yet started building its own search engine technology and relied on Moreover for its MSN Newsbot.

As we all know, the search world now belongs to Google and it is no great surprise that **Google News** has become the most popular free news search engine. It was introduced in 2002 as an English-language-only tool. From the very beginning it was different from all the earlier news search providers. It was its use of advanced clustering technologies that generated an automatically rendered news portal that set it apart. All stories about the same event were sorted together into a cluster of articles. To represent the cluster one article from the cluster was chosen and the leading passage from it was displayed, with links to all the other articles in the cluster. Surprisingly, although Google News used clustering on its news pages from the beginning, it didn't apply clustering within its search results lists until five years later, in 2007. Support for RSS subscriptions to search results came rather late as well, being introduced in 2005.

Clustering of news stories was not entirely unique to Google News, however. At Columbia University at this time there was a similar, research-oriented project called the **Columbia Newsblaster**. It had been developed by the Natural Language Processing Group led by Professor Kathy McKeown and a demo became publicly available in 2001. Just like Google News, it used article clustering, but it applied multi-document summarizing to the presentation of clusters. Where Google News was content to have one specific article serve as a source to summarize all the articles in the cluster, Columbia Newsblaster made a composite summary, using text extracts from several sources (Figure 2.4). It later offered different summaries from sources in the US, in the UK or in multiple countries.

Clustering is always language dependent and presumably this is why Google doesn't have a news search where you can cross-search over several languages. Google subsequently launched separate Google News sites in many other languages – in 2003 Google News Deutschland, Google Actualités France, Google News Italia and Google News España where launched, based on 700 German, 500 French, 250 Italian and 700 Spanish news sources respectively.

| Figure 2.4 | Columbia Newsblaster, offering automatically generated summaries from sources in different countries |

Other summaries about this story:

- Summary from United States, from articles in English (36 articles)
- Summary from multiple countries, from articles in English (40 articles)
- Summary from Canada, from articles in English (4 articles)

Other stories about vaccine, flu and Health:

- Sites in Washington area curbing swine flu vaccine clinics (11 articles)
- Government Officials Take to the Web to Address Swine Flu Fears (8 articles)
- U.S. Asks Firms to Make Swine Flu Vaccine (10 articles)

Event tracking:

- Track this story's development in time

Story keywords

vaccine, flu, Health, swine, virus

The international versions of Google News were controversial in some countries. For instance, Google had a long-standing conflict with the French news agency AFP. It was finally resolved in 2007 when Google started hosting AFP content so that it could be included in Google News. In Norway, Denmark and Belgium it has had similar problems with news publishing organizations. In the US the Washington Post decided early on that it did not want its content visible in Google News, although it later changed its mind.

In December 2006, having launched Google News in Norway the previous month, Google had to remove all news images after complaints from the newspapers and press photographers. In early 2007 a court in Belgium ruled that Google's use of republished headlines, as well as short extracts and the use of Google's cache, violated authors' rights. In order to get permission to launch its Google News Search in China, it had to remove many news sites from the results. In Denmark, Google doesn't have a news search engine at all. This is presumably because in 2002 a Danish court ruled that the news search engine NewsBooster.com illegally deep-linked to articles on the websites of news sources. A similar case in Germany in 2003 resulted in the opposite ruling, that deep-linking was to be allowed.

In 2004 a new categorizing news search engine called **Topix** was launched. Behind the newcomer was Rick Skrenta, the founder of the web directory NewHoo that became known under the name of Open Directory Project. Tired of this project, he decided that it was time to find a new way to design a news search engine. The use of categorization in Topix was geared towards creating clusters containing not single news stories but broader topics, hence the name. Topix also created clusters for companies and regions, and even for cities within the US. The concept was later expanded to include international content, extracting topics for many cities around the world. It also soon added blogs to the news sources it covered.

When Microsoft launched a new version of its MSN Search in 2005, it had been using search engine technology from Inktomi ever since 1997. Since 2005 it has been using its own in-house search technology. During 2006 a revamped search portal was introduced as Windows Live Search and included a brand new news search. The Live Search brand wasn't entirely successful and in 2009 Microsoft again presented a new search site, called Bing.com. Somewhere along the way it dropped the news search that it had developed in cooperation with Moreover.

Microsoft's current news search engine, **Bing News**, features clustering of news articles, categorized results, and RSS feeds, but no advanced search form. In August 2009 Microsoft signed an agreement with Yahoo! to provide the search engine back-end for Yahoo! for a period of 10 years. A Microsoft spokesman stated that the deal would cover web, image and video search but made no mention about news search. It seems probable that Yahoo! will keep its own news search engine for the time being.

The fourth-largest search engine in the US is **Ask.com,** which until 2006 was called AskJeeves. It originally provided a questions and answers database using natural language processing but changed its focus after acquiring the innovative search engine Teoma in 2001. In early 2008 it launched a news search engine, initially called Big News, with many new features. It uses clustering of news stories both on the home page and within search results lists, where you can filter results by categories and geographical regions.

The US is home to all the major search engines and is also the country where search engine technology originated. Many interesting news search engines have of course appeared elsewhere, but they have had a much more limited audience. In the UK the premier news search site is **NewsNow**, which has been around for a long time, having launched its real-time aggregate news headline service in 1998. It was the first British news search and is still the most interesting of the free ones in the UK. However, as a non-registered user you can search only in the headlines of articles.

In France one of the earliest news search engines was Net2One, which started in September 1999. It offered free searching for a few years, later expanding to cover several languages. Today **Wikio** is the leading news and blog search engine in France. In Germany we should mention **Paperball,** which was introduced in April 1998 and to this day continues to provide a very good index of German news websites. Another interesting German news search engine is **Romso Nachrichten,** which became available in 2005.

In January 2010 the British newspaper publisher News International Ltd, owned by the media mogul Rupert Murdoch, indirectly informed the UK news search engine NewsNow that it no longer had the right to link to articles in the online versions of *The Times* and *Sunday Times*. This was done by placing a robots.txt directive that prevented NewsNow's crawler from indexing these websites. (Robots.txt is a file, kept in the root directory of a website, that may contain instructions to prevent a search engine from indexing the website.) NewsNow protested, asking why it had been singled out and why News International hadn't banned Google News and Yahoo! News in the same way. In December 2009 NewsNow also withdrew several news sources from its subscription service, after having been unable to reach an agreement with the Newspaper Licensing Agency. It was also decided that Times Online would cease to be a free service after June 2010. Instead, subscriptions would be available at £1 a day or £2 per week. These new developments will of course present a major challenge for the free news search engines.

The best free news search engines

In the following sections our descriptions and suggestions refer to the US editions of US-based news search engines. The design and options available in other editions can sometimes vary.

Google News

The most popular news search engine, or rather news search engines, are undoubtedly Google News. We use the plural because there is actually at least one news search engine for every language that Google indexes. Google states that it has more than 40 regional editions of Google News – but while this is certainly true, there are not quite so many language versions. The different editions based on English-language content are really variations on the same news index, or at least that's how it appears to be. What differentiates them is the way the home pages are put together. Countries from a certain region have home pages on which news stories from that country and region are prominently displayed. During searching, preference is given to sources originating from the same region, which means that those results are given a higher relevance score and appear higher up in the search hits.

If you try the same search query in the various English-language editions, such as US, UK, Australia, New Zealand, Canada, South Africa, Kenya, Zimbabwe or the English edition of Google India, you will get almost exactly the same number of hits, but the results lists will differ because of the way the relevance algorithm is adapted to the region. Exactly how this works is not disclosed. The same is, of course, true for the various editions based on sources in, for instance, Spanish, Portuguese or French.

The auto-generated start pages of the different editions of Google News are dependent on the underlying clustering technology at the core of the news search engine. This technology creates a very attractive start page, giving each edition a different face adapted to the geographical region. Clustering is a very valuable feature because it's active in the search results pages as well. It provides a view of news events rather than of individual news articles and is especially convenient because of the simple fact that the same article will often be posted on numerous newspaper websites. This has to do with the fact that many news sites are wholly dependent on content originating from news agencies for their international and sometimes even national news – which means that in search engines that don't use clustering exactly the same story will appear many times within a single results list. There will of course be small variations because some parts are occasionally edited out, due to space restrictions, but you will nonetheless see many repeated headlines in the results lists from news search engines that don't use clustering. It should be pointed out that while Yahoo! News doesn't use clustering of stories, Bing News does.

In the pane on the left of the screen you can remove all the images from the stories by clicking on 'Headlines'. Conversely, you can look at only the images by clicking on 'Images'. To restore the normal appearance, click on 'All news'. There is a section to the right called 'Google Fast Flip', which will take you to the experimental Fast Flip version of Google News on the Google Labs website. Towards the bottom of the page there is also a link that allows you to return to the Standard Edition and leave your Personalized Edition of the start page – if you have taken advantage of the many ways that Google News offers to change the standard appearance.

Fast Flip provides a more graphical interface in which stories are displayed as images of the original web pages where Google News has found the articles. Below these graphics the headlines are shown in blue text. You can scan or fast-flip through the stories by clicking on the large blue arrow to the right of the previews. With each click on the arrow another batch of story images scrolls across the screen. Fast Flip is a graphically pleasing way to browse for articles, and when something grabs your attention you can click on the image to enlarge it. You can also click through to the original web page by using the link 'Read full story'. If you like Fast Flip, then you should visit **Google Labs**, where there is a version of the tool with several sections that you can customize more freely.

Now we'll take a look at the 'Advanced news search' form (see link at top of the page), which provides some interesting possibilities for tweaking your search. In the upper part, called 'Find results', there are four search boxes intended to make it easier for you to apply some basic search logic. The first one is called 'with all of the words' and is where you should enter words that should be present in all articles retrieved by the search. In the next box you can enter an exact phrase that you want to find in the texts of stories. In the third box, labelled 'with at least one of the words', you can type a list of words from which at least one should be present in the results. The fourth box allows you to specify words that should be absent from the results. This last feature can be a powerful tool for weeding out unwanted results but needs to be used with some caution. It's most effective when you get many articles that do indeed contain the words you want, but in the wrong context or with an alternative interpretation of one of your search words. In such cases you need to exclude this word and try using some other word that typically appears in the searched-for articles.

The sorting options are valuable tools and you should make good use of them (Figure 2.5). For instance, the default sorting criterion is relevance, but in news searching you are often more interested in finding the very latest news stories rather than the ones that are deemed most relevant according to some mathematical algorithm. In that case you will want to use 'Sort by date (newest first)'. On the other hand, if you want to follow stories concerning an event from the very first reports to the latest developments, use 'Sort by date (oldest first)'. The alternative 'Sort by date with duplicates included' will display the newest first, but will turn off the clustering feature. Your results list will then probably be cluttered with repetitive entries pointing to variations on the same story about the same news event. Of course, if you search for carefully chosen keywords that will generate very few hits there will probably not be any

Figure 2.5   Sorting options in Google News search

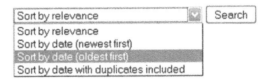

noticeable difference. If you do get annoyed by duplicate entries you can easily get rid of them by clicking 'Hide duplicates' in the pane on the left of the results page.

Returning to our exploration of the 'Advanced search form', several different types of filtering are provided in the second section of the form. The Date restriction options relate to when stories were added to the Google News index, not to the actual date of publication of the articles. Filtering by News Source is a great tool that you can use whenever you're interested in following the reporting on a particular news website. Source Location is handy if you want to restrict your search to news sources from a certain country – but how well this works is for you to discover. The same is true for the Location field, where you can let Google try to decide the relevance of different articles to the location or region that you specify. It works most of the time, but not always.

Google also tries to extract Author information and is often successful at this, but the matching frequency will never equal that of a commercial news search service. Finally, there is filtering by Occurrences. The most useful option here is searching in the headline of the article, which is a really good way to find fewer but more focused results. You have probably noticed that there's no language selection option in the advanced search form. You will of course already be in a specific edition of Google News that has a specific language, but it would have been practical to be able to change here to searching in another language. In order to do this you will first have to switch to the relevant edition of Google News.

This is actually a shortcoming in Google News, and is where Yahoo! News provides a more universal approach to news searching. In Yahoo! News you can select any language from a list of about 40, and even define a custom set of languages. With your Google News results list displayed, you can at least change from results in the language of the chosen edition to results in 'Any language' (Figure 2.6). This option, which actually reruns the search, becomes available when the results list is sorted by date. It will yield very unpractical results lists because Google News indexes so many languages. Obviously it would have been much better if you could select a small set of languages that you're familiar with.

We've already described many features of the results pages, but there are a few more that we should mention. You can restrict your search to blogs on news websites by clicking 'Blogs' in the pane on the left of the screen. You can also zoom in on a specific time frame by clicking on one of the time interval links. Other interesting things are found at the bottom of the results page. Here are links to create email alerts for your search and to create a customized section on your Google News start page. The latter uses your search query to construct this new section. Don't forget the 'RSS' link at the very bottom of any results page, which offers a feed version of your search. The 'Help' link at the bottom of the page takes you to the Google News Help Forums, where

| **Figure 2.6** | A link to show results in any language in a date-sorted Google News results list |

Sorted by relevance
› Sorted by date

› Hide duplicates
Show duplicates

Any language
› English

The international Helsinki airport, as well as the airpo reopened. All Norwegian airspace was again open. ...

Volcanic ash: Norway, **Sweden** skies shut;
Online - International News Network - 8 minutes ago
BRUSSELS: Aviation authorities say they have clos shifting winds send a new cloud of volcanic ash over

you can find answers to questions on different aspects of Google News Search. You can even suggest new features by using Google News Suggestions. To do this, click on the 'Google News' link under Google Help Forums (accessible via the 'Help' link at the bottom of the page).

Google News Archive Search

Google News Archive was launched in September 2006 and is a veritable treasure-trove that you should take your time to explore. It's not very prominently displayed on Google News and you will have to navigate to the 'Advanced search form' to access it (Figure 2.7). In the date restrictions area you will find a link to 'archive search' for articles added more than 30 days ago. Google News Archive Search has a single search box but two search mode buttons. One is for the normal archive search and the other is labelled 'Show news timeline'. Using the latter button Google will attempt to sort the stories in the results list into chronological order – otherwise it will just use the relevance algorithm. The results lists by relevance has a link to change to the Timeline view. However, in both types of results list you will get a horizontal timeline diagram showing the number of hits for different years. Click in the chart to zoom in on a specific period.

There is an 'Advanced News Archive Search' form as well, which offers some interesting ways to tailor your search. First of all you can apply basic Boolean logic using the four

Figure 2.7 The link to Google News Archive Search from the Advanced Search form

⦿ Return articles added to Google News | anytime ◇ |

◯ Return articles added to Google News between | Mar ◇ | | 23 ◇ | and | Apr ◇ | | 22 ◇ |

Try archive search for articles added more than 30 days ago

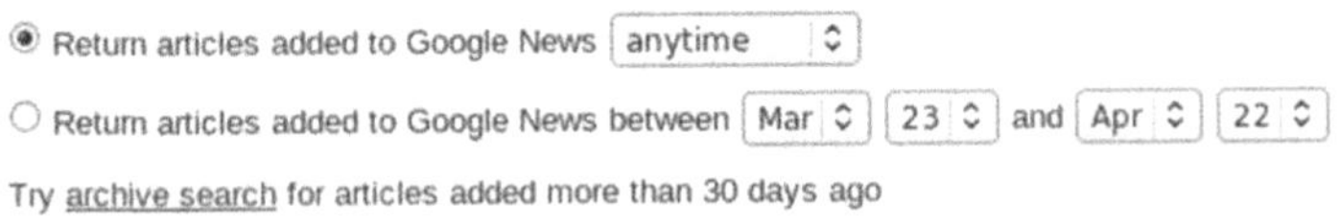

search boxes within the grey field. You can also apply Date restrictions by entering specific intervals. The date results are not always correct and shouldn't be completely trusted, but they will work most of the time. More interesting are the options for Language and to search in a specific Source. This is the only part of Google News where you can select language in the search form. You can also search in all languages. Another useful way to restrict your search is by the Price of articles. The default is to select articles of any price, but you can restrict to no price or set a maximum of $5, $10 or $50. Surprisingly, there is a choice to only include results costing at least $50! This can be used to find only the more expensive business reports.

The results lists contain a bewildering and confusing mix and there is no documentation showing which sources are included. You will also find that there is plenty of material that you must pay for if you want to read the full text. This material may reside on the websites of some of the major newspapers, such as the New York Times. In other cases it will be accessible through a third-party archive service such as ProQuestArchiver or Highbeam Research. The Los Angeles Times, the Independent (London), USA Today and the Washington Post are examples of newspapers that offer their full text in this way. Highbeam Research also has many journal articles in its extensive collection. Results such as these are labelled 'Pay Per View' and you will not always be able to see the price until you click through to the service offering the full text.

In contrast, when the full text resides on a newspaper website the price will be clearly visible in the results list. Paid articles from the New York Times normally cost $3.95, while others may cost $2.95. Full text articles that are retrieved via NewsBank, such as transcripts from the National Public Radio, the BBC Archive or Philadelphia

Inquirer normally cost the same. Articles from the French Le Monde are priced in euros and typically cost €2 apiece.

Free full text can be found on many websites but some of them may require you to register first. In such cases the text 'Free with registration' will be shown under the title of the news story. One example is content that can be found at **AccessMyLibrary.com**. There may be instances of the same article being available for free from AccessMyLibrary.com while you must pay for it using Highbeam Research. Take the time to look carefully through the results lists so as not to miss this when it happens.

With regard to the older material, some newspapers have their articles scanned and hosted by Google. This is indicated by the text 'Google News Archive' under the titles and such articles are free. The newspapers scanned by Google are mostly American. A few Canadian examples are the *Montreal Gazette*, *Toronto World* and *Ottawa Citizen*. Another example is the major Australian daily, *Sydney Morning Herald*. A fine collection with early scanned newspapers that can be accessed without cost through Google News is **PapersPast** from New Zealand. These are hosted by the National Library of New Zealand. Yet another huge free collection is transcripts from the U.S. Public Broadcasting Service.

The source that is most extensively featured of all in Google News Archive Search is the *New York Times*. Its archive of scanned articles goes all the way back to 1851, when the newspaper was founded. The early material up to the 1920s is free, but then comes a period up to the mid 1980s where you must pay for the articles. This still leaves an incredible amount of amazing reading that can be done all for free. For instance, you can read an account of the funeral of the explorer Dr David Livingstone in 1874, or early reports of the *Titanic* disaster in 1912.

Yahoo! News

In April 2010 Yahoo! launched a new look for its News Search in which some of its advanced features were not initially available. During the spring of 2010 Microsoft and Yahoo! began to implement a search alliance in which Microsoft will provide the underlying search technology for a period of 10 years. Their agreement covers web, image and video search but makes no explicit mention of news search. Consequently, we have yet to learn what this alliance will mean for the development of Yahoo! News. At the time of writing the front page of the US version of Yahoo! News shows news headlines for the top stories, the most popular stories and 15 or so different subject categories. The most popular stories are divided into Most Emailed, Most Viewed and Most Recommended. The subject categories include, among others World News, U.S. News, Politics, Science, Entertainment, Sports and also Odd News and Opinion. The source for the headlines displayed for each category defaults to articles from Associated Press – for all but Odd News, which uses Reuters, and Opinion, which uses Csmonitor.com.

There is no attempt to cluster news stories, but if you don't like the headlines from the default source you can choose other sources instead. For instance, for World News you may choose from Reuters, AFP, Time, NPR and a few more. There is a strong emphasis on news agency material, as has been the case from the very beginning of Yahoo! News. To search the news index you have to use the search box on the left, just below the menu bar, not the one at the top right of the screen, which will run your search in the normal web index. There are four choices for the news search: you can search in either All News, Yahoo! News Only, News Photos or Video/Audio. Most people will probably just enter their search words without bothering about this.

As you type you will get suggestions for keywords and phrases and many times there will be something that matches your intentions. The results lists show the hits from News Images and News Videos on top, with the text results below. Looking at the source names for articles, photos and videos you will see many that are labelled like this: 'AP via Yahoo! News' or 'Reuters via Yahoo! News'. This is because some of the content is actually hosted by Yahoo!, rather than being indexed from the web. When you restrict your search to Yahoo! News Only, or News Photos, or Video/Audio the results will come from the hosted sources.

By default, search results are ordered by relevance and the only other option is to sort them by time. Sorting by time is important if you want to use the RSS feed version of your search in a feed reader so as to monitor your search topic. If you want to subscribe to your search using the My Yahoo! reader you can do so using the button labelled 'Get updates' in the square to the right of the results. You can also subscribe to searches using email alerts. These can be delivered once a day or continuously 'as they happen'. You should think twice before choosing the latter!

You can set several interesting preferences in Yahoo! News. For example, the search suggestions can be tweaked by editing the so-called Search Assist Layer Frequency. You can disable suggestions completely, show suggestions whenever they are available, or have them jump in only if you appear to need assistance. The Advanced Search form in Yahoo! News has recently become available again. It is fairly similar to the one in Google News, with the same search boxes for basic Boolean search logic and the option for searching in headlines. You can also filter by selecting a specific source or selecting a set of languages from which to include the results (not available in Google News).

Filtering of search results in Yahoo! News is now also available on the results pages. This follows a general trend in the present evolution of search interfaces: the old-school advanced search forms have started to disappear and many interesting filtering options have appeared in the results views. It is true that very few people use advanced search forms, but it doesn't hurt to have them available for those who find them useful. In our opinion it's very important to have advanced search options available for power users, who tend to use search tools more frequently – and are also the ones who often write, talk, teach and recommend tools to other users. In our opinion it's essential not to neglect the needs of more experienced users, even though they are clearly in a minority.

You can find the new filtering options in Yahoo! News in the pane on the left of the results page. Here you will find a list of the sources that contain the most hits (Figure 2.8). It seems that a maximum of 10 sources can be displayed. Unfortunately all of the sources that are hosted by Yahoo! News are lumped

Figure 2.8 **The new filtering by news source in Yahoo! News results lists**

◎ CBS News (828)

◎! Yahoo! News (366)

⬤ ABC News (325)

🅑 Bloomberg (249)

◎! Yahoo! Finan... (145)

𝓔 New York Tim... (97)

🅕 Fox News (89)

🆂🆆 BusinessWeek (80)

🌐 Washington P... (67)

🦅 MSNBC (66)

Iceland Volcano - News Image

1,258 News Images

Millions watch **Iceland volcano** eru
Millions of people around the world have be
of **Iceland**'s Eyjafjjoell **volcano** minute-to-r
through webcams transmitting the activity I
AFP via Yahoo! News - Apr 22 8:58 AM

together, which means that stories from news agencies such as AP, AFP and Reuters can't be displayed separately.

Two other post-search filtering options are currently available. These are Filter by Type and Filter by Time. The types are the default All, Images and Video. If you choose Images and Video you will get results from sources that are hosted by Yahoo! News and they are labelled 'via Yahoo! News'. The time filter allows you to restrict to content from the past hour, day or week. It will be interesting to follow how the new Yahoo! News develops.

Topix

Topix indexes some 50,000 news and blog sources and has been on the top 10 list of news destinations compiled by ComScore. The core technology underlying Topix is the use of artificial intelligence algorithms to sort articles into one or more of the 360,000 topical news pages that have been generated using clustering technology. The other distinguishing feature is the way in which you can participate in discussions about news stories. You can comment on any story displayed in Topix, and many people do – according to Topix, more than 30,000 comments are made every day. There are also the popular forums where you can engage in discussions on almost any news topic.

On the Topix home page you will be offered news within your local area because Topix attempts to automatically discover where the connecting computer is located. If you're not happy with the choice you can click on 'Change City'. Because Topix tries to detect your geographical location and adapt to it, your own encounter with it may not be fully consistent with the description that we provide here. Local news is shown in the section on the left of the screen, where you are offered the most recent stories and the most commented-on stories of interest in your region. Comments are written by other Topix visitors and you can comment on stories yourself using the 'Comment' link. Topix has a very active community, as you can see from the comments counter at the bottom of the page.

Below the local news section of the home page you have a search box, followed by the Top Stories, which presents the current 10 top news stories. By clicking on any of the stories you can get an extended view that shows more articles in the cluster making up the story topic. You will also get pointers to other stories concerning the more general topic to which the story belongs. At the top right of the story are a chart showing the past week's news activity for the country from which the story comes and links to other news from that country. And at the foot of the story a link takes you to the discussion forums for the general topic to which the story belongs. Clicking on the heading 'Top Stories' at the top of this section extends the entire section. To the right of the Top Stories section 'News Trends' presents a set of charts and links to the 'hottest' news topics of the past seven days.

At the top right of the home page is the search box (there is also a search box separating the local news section from the Top Stories section), where you can enter keywords or zip codes. The latter option will be useful mostly for US residents. As you type in the search box various topic suggestions appear, arranged in groups such as People, Entertainment, Sports, Places and others. The results are displayed in the middle column of the screen in chronological order, with the newest stories first, with your search words highlighted (if you choose a topic suggestion rather than submitting a search, the search words that you typed will not be highlighted). There doesn't seem to be any way to sort results by relevance.

When you submit a search using your own words, rather than choosing a topic suggestion that is offered during the search, you will get an Advanced Search form to the right of the results lists, where you can refine your search or submit a new search (Figure 2.9). The form allows you to restrict your search to blogs or exclude blogs from the results. You can also restrict the results by source, URL or geographical location. Any results page can be subscribed to using the feed link in the address bar at the top of the screen; there is no need to sort results by date before you subscribe because they are already sorted in this way.

Figure 2.9 The Advanced Search form in Topix can be found next to the results list

Advanced Search

Search All Topics

Keyword(s)

balotelli

Blog search

News and Blogs ⬍

Restrict to source

For example: CNN, Newsday, Fox Sports, New York Times, etc.

Restrict to URL

For example: cnn.com, newsday.com, foxsports.com, nytimes.com, etc.

Restrict to ZIP code or city

For example: 94303 or New York, NY

Search All Topics

Bing News

To access Bing News in Microsoft's Bing search engine click on the 'News' link on the left of the screen, which takes you to the news search home page. To use the US version, which is described here, you may have to click on the link 'Go to Bing in the United States', which is at the foot of the screen. The top news stories are organized into nine subject categories, such as Top Stories, World, Business, Politics, etc. By clicking on any of the category tabs at the top of the screen you can display the top nine stories for that category. Each story is clustered and by clicking 'More on this story' you can find more articles on the same topic (Figure 2.10). Each page also offers some video links. A link on the right, just below the category tabs, provides an option to view only news videos. Each news category page has its own RSS feed that you can subscribe to; the link for this is also under the category tabs.

If you click on 'Settings' in the top right corner of the screen you can access a range of settings that can be altered to suit your needs. By default, Bing News searches for articles in any language, but you can change to a selection of languages of your own choice. You can also change the language of Bing's display from English to one of the other 40 or so languages available. If you don't like the search suggestions that are displayed as you type your keywords you can turn this feature off. And if you think you aren't

Figure 2.10 Clustered articles in Bing News can be accessed by clicking 'More on this story'

Amorous slug, orange snake among finds on Borneo

KUALA LUMPUR, Malaysia — A lungless frog, a frog that flies and a slug that shoots love darts are among 123 new species found in Borneo since 2007 in a project to conserve one of the oldest rain forests in the world. A report by the global...
comcast.net · 51 minutes ago

New animal species discovered in Borneo · YAHOO!
Rare Borneo rhino caught on camera in Malaysia · Examiner

More on this story

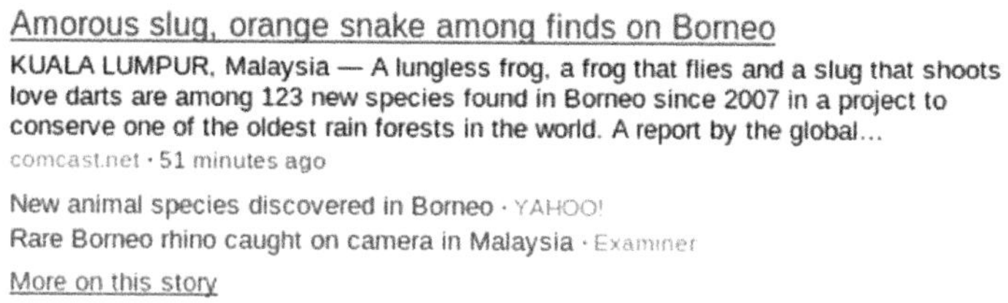

getting all the hits that you want you can try disabling the SafeSearch filter (by default, it's set to Moderate).

Unfortunately Bing News doesn't provide an advanced search form and Help pages don't document any special search syntax (to find Help, go to the very bottom of the screen). In fact Bing seems to have a lot fewer features when compared to Microsoft's earlier Live Search engine. However, there are some helpful post-search filtering options, displayed to the left of the search results.

Related Searches enables you to search for related topics. These related searches are apparently generated using a technology called named entity recognition (NER) and they often feature personal names and names of places or organizations. You may see a few mistakes being made by the NER engine, but it does provide valuable assistance in many cases. The 'See Also' links are good for finding mentions of the search words in blog posts and on Twitter.

Other news search engines

Rocketnews used to provide a full-featured news search engine that was freely available. Since its acquisition by management consultant Murray Owens in 2008, the focus is now more oriented towards business search for paying customers. It still maintains a free search function, but this is very basic and without any useful extra tools or advanced search form. Rocketnews has a typical collection of subject categories, with stories mostly from news agencies such as AP, AFP and Reuters. Each category has its own RSS feed and you can also receive search results as RSS feeds.

A very capable news search engine is **NewsNow**, from the UK. Free searching is available only in article headlines and news feed titles. How useful you find NewsNow will depend on whether headline searching is sufficient for your needs. Even if it isn't, you can still make use of NewsNow by browsing its many news categories. It offers a vast number of topics that are hierarchically sorted and easily accessible via a well-designed interface that is fascinating to explore. For paying customers, NewsNow delivers subscription services that offer tailored search feeds or pre-built topical feeds compiled from its more than 39,000 sources in 20 languages from 141 countries.

Highbeam Research is an article database covering more than 6,500 publications, among which are many interesting news sources. It's especially strong in international news wire content and covers newspapers from many countries. Most of the content is not available for free, but Highbeam can still be used as an excellent news search engine in which you can specify the news source of your search (Figure 2.11). To take just one example, it has an archive of 2.8 million PR Newswire releases going back to 1989. When you find articles that you want to read, you can either use Highbeam's free 7-day trial or try to find the same articles on the free web.

FindArticles is another popular article database that offers some free content, and much more that you have to pay for.

Figure 2.11 The handy publications search feature in the Highbeam Research Advanced Search form

FindArticles was originally created in 2000 by the web directory company Looksmart but was subsequently sold to Cnet, which is now a part of CBS Interactive. You should be aware that FindArticles as well as Highbeam Research includes a whole lot more than just news sources. Both index a great many specialized journals and magazines that are not news related.

Directories of news sites

Many of the bigger newspapers offer unlimited searching and/or browsing of their archives, while you have to pay for the full text. However, some will let you read articles from a limited time period for free. Some even offer everything they ever published for free, like the German weekly *Die Zeit*. To find the websites of the bigger newspapers in different countries you can use a directory such as **Newslink.org**, which has maintained an excellent directory of news sites since 2002. Another good choice is the newspaper directory of the **IPL2**, which resulted from a merger between the renowned Internet Public Library and the Librarians' Internet Index. Or you may want to use **ABYZ NewsLinks**, which is an extensive collection of links to different news sites and which has been around since 2000. Even older is **The Paperboy**, run by Australian travel writer Ian Duckworth, who started listing news sites in late 1997 and is still at it with the help of his brother Andrew. The Dutch **Kidon Media-Link** is yet another independent news directory that started with a few bookmarks in 1994, evolved into a link database in 1998 and now contains almost 20,000 news links. You can also find extensive collections of links to news websites in the major web directories **Open Directory Project** and the **Yahoo! Directory**.

Major newspapers with web archives

While you will normally be able to read the news articles of the current week or the last 14 days on the websites of newspapers, access to older material is another story. Many of the major US newspapers, such as USA Today, the Wall Street Journal, Washington Post and Los Angeles Times, provide access to archived articles through **ProQuestArchiver** – but certainly not for free. The San Francisco Chronicle, Chicago Tribune, San Diego Source and Seattle Times are examples of newspapers that offer several years of free archives on their own websites. The New York Times is exceptional in offering many decades of material without charge.

A good list of US newspaper archives on the web is maintained by the **Special Library Association's (SLA) News Division.** Here you can look up which newspapers have archives, whether they offer any free access and for what years. SLA has a separate list of international news archives on the web but it has been only partially updated since 2004. **Wikipedia** has a list of newspaper archives that covers several countries and this is updated more frequently. Even better is the extensive list maintained by the **International Coalition of Newspapers** (ICON), which has very broad international coverage. The ICON list is probably the best starting place for most users with a non-US focus. While we have focused here on free news search, below we provide a few examples of the charges for access to the full text of archived stories.

In the UK the **Daily Telegraph** has a generous policy and has an archive which provides free access to all articles from June 2000 onwards. The **Independent** is even more friendly and will let you browse and read all articles from 1992. The **Financial Times** offers 10 free articles per 30-day period once you have completed a registration. **The Times Online Archive** currently offers a few selected articles without charge and you can search its full content for free going all the way back to 1785! You can purchase a day pass for £4.95 if you need to access just a few articles. If you need to do more research that will require a little more time a monthly membership for £14.95 can be a good choice. The selected articles on the front page of the archive are often interesting and can be very entertaining reading. The archives of the **Guardian** and the **Observer** don't display any sample reading on the home page but if you go to the Digital Archive page there are some there. This archive is somewhat pricier than the Times and offers day passes for £7.95 and 3-day access for £14.95.

Die Zeit is a German weekly of very high quality and offers all its articles for free, from its start back in 1946 (Figure 2.12). Articles prior to 1994 have been scanned and indexed using OCR. **Die Welt** is one of the biggest German dailies; it has a free archive search and will let you read all articles from 1995 without charge. **Frankfurt Allgemeine Zeitung** offers archived articles for €2 each and you can choose between an HTML version and an image of the newspaper page. **Süddeutsche Zeitung** is a bit cheaper, charging €1.50 to view a single article for 24 hours. Alternatively you can download a PDF of the original news page that contains the article. From **Berliner Morgenpost** you can't buy individual articles; instead you have to pay for 30 days of access, but it will set you back only €4.95. For €8 a month you can read up to 30 archived articles from the French **Le Figaro**. Its competitor **Le Monde** is slightly cheaper at €6 for 25 archived articles. Other bigger dailies in France might allow you to buy single articles, like **Sud Ouest**, which charges €2 per article or €12.50 for 10.

Figure 2.12	Finding articles by individual authors in the free archives of *Die Zeit* isn't difficult

B AUTORENREGISTER

A B C D E F G H I J K L M N O P Q R S T U V W X Y Z

Bachmann, Stefanie RSS

Bader, Katarina RSS

Bader, Reiner RSS

Baecker, Dirk RSS

Baer, Matthias RSS

Baer-Bogenschütz, Dorothee RSS

Blumenfeld, Erik RSS

Blümner, Heike RSS

Blüthmann, Heinz RSS

Bneau, Elisabeth RSS

Bobew, A.P. RSS

Bobic, Fredi RSS

Broadcast news

ABC News has a very clean and neatly designed archive search that will let you retrieve material for free going back to 1999. Results can be refined in various ways according to type, such as stories, photos, videos and blogs, or by dates, sections or shows. Videos are normally preceded by a short commercial. Results can be sorted with the oldest first, which can be desirable at times. Most-viewed, most-commented and most-emailed stories are on display, but not so prominently. ABC News also offers a large selection of RSS feeds of topical news, most popular news, blogs and videos.

CBS News also has an extensive archive going back to 1999, with content free of charge. There are several handy ways to narrow down your search results from within the results list. You can choose media types such as stories, blogs, videos or photo essays. Limits by specific date intervals are possible and there are many different Types by which to limit, with a long list of subjects, sections and categorized content from AP. You can also select from a list of Shows (which has similar categories to the Types), including of course the famous ones such as '60 Minutes', 'The Early Show' and 'Face The Nation'. The most-viewed stories and the most-commented are shown on the right of the screen. The page that lists a selection of CBS News RSS feeds offers easy subscription using My Yahoo!, Newsgator and Netvibes.

CNN relies on Google for its search facility and it is not nearly as effective as the search on ABC News or CBS News. Results are categorized merely as Stories and Videos and can be sorted by date or relevance. There is an Advanced Search where you can at least choose from 10 different sections and do some date restrictions, but it covers only the last 12 months. To find the older articles you have to go manually through the results pages, backwards in time. CNN has a special feature called NewsPulse, which is labelled as a beta version and is accessible via a tab in the US edition. It provides lists of the most popular news for a selection of time periods ranging from the last 15 minutes to the last 30 days. There are about 20 RSS feeds but the only choice of reader for easy subscription is My Yahoo!.

It's no surprise that **MSNBC News** uses Bing from Microsoft for its search, but it's also very basic in comparison to ABC News and CBS News. In fact you can't do any filtering at all or sort the results in any way, and the only choices are Articles or Images. The results lists are ordered only by relevance, which is very awkward if you don't have very specific search terms. However, the archive does seem to go back several years. There are 17 RSS channels and about the same number of video and audio podcasts that you can subscribe to.

Fox News has its own search engine with many options for filtering results. You can refine by date, by content type, by categories and by sections. Fox News offers a great many RSS feeds for news categories, blogs, a few columns and a host of different video feeds. It also offers RSS feeds for searches – a very powerful tool if you follow Fox News regularly. If you want to subscribe to the feeds there are 13 different readers to choose from, so the chances are good that your favourite will be among them.

In addition to the websites of the commercial networks there are the US public service broadcasters **PBS** (Public Broadcasting Service) and **NPR** (National Public Radio). They both have very extensive archives and great websites that are a pleasure to explore. They are particularly strong in educational content and have many interactive activities. NPR has an impressive number of podcasts that you can subscribe to and its podcast directory lists hundreds of podcasts from its own stations and its over 50 partner radio stations.

The British **BBC News** has excellent international coverage and features regional news portals for Africa, South Asia, the Middle East and other regions. It has an extensive archive going way back into the 1990s. The BBC was among the earliest adopters of RSS technology and now offers about 15 news feeds and 8 video feeds. There are not a lot of search features, however, and results can be filtered only by choosing News & Sport or TV & Radio Programmes. Unfortunately, results cannot be sorted by date.

BBC Worldwide has a wonderful website called **BBC Motion Gallery** with a large collection of video footage not only from the BBC but also from broadcasters such as CBS, NHK (Japan), CCTV (China) and ABC (Australia). The films are of outstanding quality and the site has a very good search engine. Results can be filtered by format, footage type, content type, rights management and release status. There is an embedded player on the results pages that automatically starts playing the clips when you hover the cursor over the clip. If the kids are acting up, search for tiger or some other animal and they are likely to sit glued to the screen ... for at least a little while.

The Canadian Broadcasting Corporation, CBC, has a dedicated archive site called **CBC Digital Archive** with some amazing content. This radio and TV archive goes back several decades. Using the Date tab in the Advanced Search form you can find more than 50 radio clips from the 1930s alone – and one from 1927. There are several ways to browse and search the archives, such as by people, activities, programmes and of course keyword. Maybe you want to listen to an interview with the famous singer-songwriter Joni Mitchell from 1967, or a young Mario Lemieux in 1989, or Leonard Cohen in 1966, or even a 13-year-old Wayne Gretzky? It's all available in the CBC Archives. There is also a French **Radio-Canada Digital Archives** with equally impressive content.

In Germany several regional broadcasting corporations cooperate to produce the national television channel ARD. The **ARD news portal** is a good place to start looking for German news. The search engine covers several of the larger TV and radio stations, such as Norddeutschen Rundfunk, Bayerische Rundfunk, Radio Bremen, Rundfunk Berlin-Brandenburg and Deutschlandradio. There is also a second national German news channel called **ZDF** which is run by the regional governments. It has an extensive Mediathek and many archived stories that can be read for free. Look for the advanced search form, called Erweiterte Suche.

News agencies

The big international news agencies produce material that is republished all over the web, but their offerings can be meagre on their own websites. The leading American news agency is **Associated Press** (AP), which traces its roots all the way back to 1846. AP doesn't offer a lot at its corporate website but you can search its very latest headlines and find full stories for some of them. It's far better to access its recent content via Google News or Yahoo! News. That way you can find a whole month's worth of AP articles and read them all for free.

The other American news agency, **United Press International** (UPI), has a much more generous website with lots of full content available. Its archived stories can also be read for free and the material goes back several years. Particularly interesting is the audio archive, where you can listen to annual Year in Review highlights from UPI radio, starting in 1959 and going up to 1994. There's also a Spanish version of the UPI website. UPI recently celebrated its 100th anniversary, having been in operation since 1907.

Reuters is the largest British news agency, but was founded by a German called Paul Reuter, in 1851. Incidentally, the original name of this seminal figure in the world of news was Israel Bere Josafat and his father was a Jewish rabbi. One of the modes of transmission used by Reuter was by carrier pigeons flying between Aachen and Brussels. Reuter soon started using the newly invented telegraph and relocated to London. Reuters has a very good web presence offering 16 regional editions and with extensive content available. The last two months of stories, photos and videos are searchable and can be read and watched for free. Reuters currently offers 18 RSS feeds and 9 podcasts that you can subscribe to.

The French **Agence France-Press** (AFP) is the oldest news agency in the world. It was started 1835 in Paris as Agence Havas and one of its early employees was a certain Paul Reuter. Today it is one of the three largest English-language news agencies, together with AP and Reuters. Its website offers nothing in the way of news search. AFP had a long conflict with Google and withheld its content from the

Google news search engine for several years. Nowadays they are on more friendly terms and Google hosts AFP content, so Google News is a good place to search for and read AFP stories from the last 30 days. Its articles in French are available through the Google Actualités search engine.

Germany's biggest news agency is **Deutsche Presse-Agentur** (DPA) and was launched in 1949. It has news services in German, English, Spanish and Arabic. It doesn't provide any search facilities on its own websites but its content is indexed by Yahoo! Nachricthen. You can enter DPA as the source in the Advanced Search form and search for DPA articles from there. Of course, DPA is also syndicated to many of the German newspapers and its stories are republished on their websites. Another big German news agency is **Deutscher Depeschen Dienst** (DDP), which was started by former UPI staff in Germany in 1971 and later incorporated the state-controlled East German agency ADN. DDP stories can also be found using Yahoo! Nachrichten and the abbreviation DDP can be used in the source field to search for them.

The official government-controlled news agency of Russia is **ITAR-TASS**. It has a long history going back to 1904, when the St Petersburg Telegraph Agency was set up. It has gone through many name changes and survived the Soviet era as the central news agency. ITAR-TASS has a news portal in English that offers a lot of material, and a search engine that will let you retrieve stories going back a year or so. The articles in English are indexed by Google News as well. An independent non-governmental Russian news agency that produces high-quality material is **Interfax**. Starting from 1989, it provides deep coverage of Russia, its Eurasian neighbours and China.

The Japanese news agency Kyodo has an English-language website called **Kyodo News**. Here you can browse the latest headlines for different subjects and for special sections such as obituaries and North Korea. However, you can read only the opening sentences of the articles for free. The state-controlled Chinese **Xinhua News Agency** has a news portal in English called China View. Using this you can read Xinhua's full stories, search its archives back to 2001 and find the addresses of its eight RSS feeds in English. An important TV station and news agency that plays a central role in the Arabic world is **Al Jazeera**. It has a well-designed news portal in English with a huge amount of free content and also offers an RSS feed. Its search engine will let you retrieve all its articles from 2003 onwards.

Asian news agencies are excellently covered by **Highbeam Research**. You can search articles for free in Highbeam and limit to specific sources, but you can't read more than the beginning of the text. Its archives are outstanding and cover Xinhua since 1995, Yonhap (Korea), Pakistan Press International, Press Trust of India, Antara (Indonesia) and United News of Bangladesh since 2003 and Vietnamese News Agency and Philippines News Agency since 2008. Highbeam also indexes several of the smaller news agencies from other Asian countries and a few regional wires such as Asian News International (ANI) and Asia Pulse News.

You should be aware of the existence of the so-called alternative news agencies. These operate differently from the commercial news agencies and can have a more critical and often political content. One of the most interesting is **Inter Press Service** (IPS), which often provides an alternative view of news events and aims to tell the underlying story. Another independent news agency worth mentioning is **Indymedia**. It describes itself as 'a collective of independent media organizations and hundreds of journalists offering grassroots, non-corporate coverage. Indymedia is a democratic media outlet for the creation of radical, accurate, and passionate tellings of truth.' While some may argue that it is politically biased, others may feel that it is independent and free from commercial interests.

Press release wires

The two most important international press release wires are PR Newswire and Business Wire. Both are American and have a long history, with PR Newswire starting in 1954 and Business Wire in 1961. They provide direct wires to news agencies, broadcast networks and media companies all round the world. Their content is indexed by all the big news search engines and they have their own websites where you can search and browse the latest press releases.

PR Newswire has a searchable archive of 180 days, and using the Advanced Search you can limit by industries, subjects and US states. It offers a large number of topical RSS feeds, categorized according to industries and markets. PR Newswire also publishes press releases in Spanish, Portuguese and Chinese and has regional sites with content from Asia, Brazil, the UK and Europe, Canada, China and France. On the **Business Wire** website you can restrict searches to headlines, tickers, company names and ISINs (International Securities Identification Numbers). The search only covers the latest month, but Business Wire has news in many more languages than PR Newswire. The RSS feeds are categorized by industries, subjects and languages. Another large English-language press release service is **PRWeb** through which you can publish press releases at a low cost, and which is therefore used by many smaller businesses. It is very well indexed by the news search engines.

To search for older press releases you normally have to use one of the commercial services or Highbeam Research.

However, many corporate websites have free archives of press releases that have been published through PR Newswire, Business Wire or the newer **Market Wire**. The latter was originally called Internet Wire and was launched in 1994. Another good way to find older press releases is by looking at older versions of corporate websites that have been archived in the **Internet Archive**. Here you can find many press releases from companies that have gone out of business or have been acquired by larger corporations. This can be a time-consuming task at times, but remember, you can save a lot of money by using the Internet Archive in this way.

Generally speaking, the best way to monitor the press release wires is through the news search engines, where you can conduct keyword searches and restrict your results to a specific source such as PR Newswire or Business Wire. You can then sort the results by date and grab the URL for the feed version of the search. The third-biggest press release wire is **M2 Presswire** in the UK but its website provides only the very latest releases for search and just a handful of feeds. Unfortunately, releases from M2 Presswire are not very well covered by the news search engines and material from M2 is probably best monitored using a professional search service. If you just want to search their releases you can do so in Highbeam Research, which has an excellent archive of more than 800,000 M2 press releases.

In Germany there is an excellent website called **Presse-portal** where you can read press releases from the largest German release service, Ots (Originaltextservice). The portal is maintained by NewsAktuell, a subsidiary of the biggest German news agency, DPA. The archive at Presseportal goes back to 2001 and all releases can be read without charge. The search interface provides an option for searching within your search results, which is convenient if you get too many hits. News images from the Obs (Originalbildservice) are included in the search results. Presseportal also offers a comprehensive collection of RSS feeds. Using Yahoo! Nachrichten you can search for keywords and specify Ots as the source (Quelle) and save the result page (sorted by date) as an RSS feed.

A great website in France for press releases is the press portal **Categorynet,** which was created in 1998 by Greg Manset. The original plan to sell journalistic content produced by a team of freelance writers didn't survive the dot.com crash and Categorynet became a dedicated press and PR portal with a large community. Here you can find French-language press releases and press rooms for many companies and organizations. Press releases can be read for free and the archives can be searched using the Google-powered search engine. You can also browse the press releases, which are categorized by many different topics. Categorynet offers a large selection of topical RSS feeds of press releases and has many active discussion forums. Keyword-based RSS search feeds can be created in the French Google Actualités by entering Categorynet as the Source d'information in the Advanced Search form.

One of the biggest press release services to focus on European distribution is the **Hugin Group,** which now belongs to ThomsonReuters. It has an excellent archive search on its own website, with an extensive back archive and search interfaces in eleven European languages (click on the little flag icon at the top right to see the available languages). You will also find press rooms for many European companies and organizations at Hugin Online. One of the newer press release services is **Asia Business News** or the ABN Newswire, which was launched in 2005. It has quickly become a leader in the Australasian region, with releases published in simplified and traditional Chinese, Korean, Japanese, Arabic and English. Other important press release services in Asia are the **Japan Corporate News (JCN) Newswire** and the **Korea Newswire**. They both have very good websites in English, with search engines and archives. ABN Newswire and JCN Newswire are also indexed by Highbeam – you can use its advanced search form for more search options and then find the full text for free on the ABN and JCN websites.

Scientific wires

Scientific news stories are normally connected to the publication of articles in peer-reviewed scientific journals. Within the scientific community there is always a race to publish your findings first in any given area, so many new discoveries are typically kept more or less secret until the day of publication of the articles. This means that many of the scientific press releases often coincide with the publication of a journal issue. Sometimes articles are published electronically on the websites of journals before they appear in the printed versions. Some scientific journals have their own table-of-contents alerts and RSS feeds that you can subscribe to. Scientific bibliographic databases such as **Web of Science, Scopus** and **Engineering Village** are normally fee based, but many university libraries subscribe to them and you can access them from the public computers in campus libraries. They also feature RSS feeds based on keyword searches and, once you have created a search, you can subscribe to it from a feed reader outside the campus.

The biggest press release service for science news is **EurekAlert,** which is operated by the American Association for the Advancement of Science. EurekAlert has a search engine that lets you search its archive going back to its start in 1996. It has an excellent browsing feature from which you can select very specific areas of interest. Similar wire services, but with smaller coverage, are **Newswise**, the European **AlphaGalileo** and the German **Informationsdienst Wissenschaft** (IDW). Excellent coverage of science can also be found at **NewScientist.com**, **BBC News Science** and **ScienceNews**. The leading academic journals *Nature* and *Science* have their own news websites with a limited selection of free content.

ScienceDaily doesn't so much publish press releases as act as an aggregator of scientific releases from all kinds of sources. Its coverage is therefore much greater than that of any of the individual press release services. It's an excellent one-stop shop for science news releases. It has its own RSS feed and also produces several newsletters. News search engines such as Google News index the major science wires, including ScienceDaily, and you can use it to set up keyword monitoring in feed form.

Historical newspaper digitizing projects

Nowadays there are a great many newspaper digitizing projects all round the world. Some of them offer amazing treasures that can be explored all for free. Indeed the great quantity of scanned newspaper pages from the nineteenth and early twentieth centuries is starting to form a vast public-domain corpus available to historical researchers. Many of these ambitious projects are being performed by national libraries, regional central libraries, academic libraries and sometimes even by smaller public libraries. Several initiatives on a national scale are under way and the future for finding old news stories is looking very bright. Here are some examples of what you can dig into right now.

We have already mentioned several US archives in connection to Google News Archive Search and you can find many more using the lists suggested, so now we'll take a look at the rest of the English-speaking world. In the UK there are not so many free newspaper archives to be found. The British Library has a carefully selected collection of 49 titles called **British Newspapers 1800–1900**. However, only two titles are offered for free and to view the articles from the other titles you need to purchase either a 24-hour pass or a 7-day pass. **Gazettes Online**, on the other hand, is an intriguing and entirely free collection, covering a 350-year period, of the London, Edinburgh and Belfast editions of *The Gazette*. The Gazettes are the official government record of regulatory and legal information and therefore quite unlike any normal newspaper. This fantastic resource for professional historians and hobbyists has an advanced search interface with an interesting feature: you can select from a list of 16 major historic events and be pointed to the relevant issues covering them. In issue 85 for 10 September 1666, for instance, you can read how the authorities in Whitehall described the Great Fire of London. Looking for something a little more recent, you can go to issue 49194 and read the reports from the 1982 Falklands War.

We've already mentioned the newspaper archive of the National Library of New Zealand, called PapersPast, in connection with Google News. A similar resource is available in Australia, called **NLA Australian Newspapers**. Launched by the National Library of Australia in August 2009, it currently covers 37 titles and a period from 1803 to 1954. A total of more than 16 million articles are all searchable, although the quality of the OCR processing isn't perfect (the same can of course be said of many of these archives). The interface is very easy to navigate; the OCR text is displayed on the left and the newspaper image on the right, so you can easily compare the two. There is a good Advanced Search form that allows you to search in headlines and captions and restrict by various article lengths.

The **Irish Newspaper Archives** covers 19 newspapers and many more are coming. It has very good descriptions of the available newspapers and goes back to 1763. Its ambitious goal is to create a complete archive of all historical Irish newspapers, so stay tuned. In **Canada** there is no central newspaper archive, but there are several good regional collections from, for instance Alberta, British Columbia and Manitoba. The official newspaper of the government of Canada is called the *Canada Gazette*. More than 80 per cent of its content from 1841 onwards is already available, even though the digitization project started as recently as 2007.

A part of the vast **Gallica Bibliothèque Numérique** created by the Bibliothèque National de France in Paris is dedicated to periodical publications. In this collection there is a fine selection of daily newspapers (*la presse quotidienne*) which includes *Le Figaro* (1826–40, 1854–1942), *La Presse* (1836–1924), *Le Temps* (1861–1939), *L' Humanité* (1904–39) and, from the Napoleonic era, *Journal de L'Empire* (1805–14). In Spain the Biblioteca Nacional de España makes almost 200 historical newspaper titles available via its **Hemeroteca Digital**. There are several great regional and local collections as well, covering, for example, Barcelona, Andalusia, Galicia, Gijón and Castilla-La Mancha.

In **Germany** there are several regional newspaper archive collections, typically started by the larger libraries of the different regions. Some examples are the digitization projects of the Bayerische Landesbibliothek, Universitätsbibliothek Heidelberg, Universitätsbibliothek Augsburg and the Sächsische Landesbibliothek in collaboration with Staats- und Universitätsbibliothek Dresden. The Staatsbibliothek zu

Berlin hosts **Die Digitale Bibliothek**, containing the largest collection, with more than 70 titles. Don't forget the online archives of the weekly *Die Zeit* that we mentioned earlier, which covers all of its issues, starting in 1946.

In the **Historical Newspaper Library** of the National Library of Finland you will find all of the newspapers that were published between 1771 and 1900. This vast collection contains 1.7 million newspaper pages that can all be read for free, using an excellent interface. Not only that, the complete issues can be downloaded free of charge as PDF files. Being from Sweden, we should not fail to mention that the oldest newspaper in the world that is still published is *Post-och Inrikes Tidningar*, which was founded by Queen Victoria of Sweden in 1645. Since 2007, however, it has been published only in electronic format. The National Library of Sweden has scanned a great deal of this newspaper's content from the nineteenth century and we have made some interesting genealogical discoveries in this collection (Figure 2.13).

Figure 2.13 Using microfilm to discover the tragic circumstances of the death of an ancestor. (From *Norrländska Korrespondenten*, 3 December 1856)

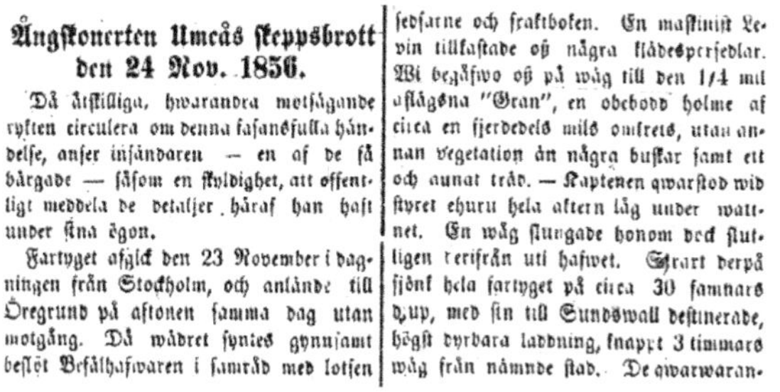

Ångskonerten Umeås skeppsbrott den 24 Nov. 1856.

Då åtskilliga, hwarandra motsägande rykten circulera om denna fasansfulla händelse, anser insändaren — en af de få bärgade — såsom en skyldighet, att offentligt meddela de detaljer, häraf han haft under sina ögon.

Fartyget afgick den 23 November i dagningen från Stockholm, och anlände till Öregrund på aftonen samma dag utan motgång. Då wädret syntes gynnsamt beslöt Befälhafwaren i samråd med lotsen sedlarne och fraktboken. En maskinist Levin tillkastade oss några klädespersedlar. Wi begåfwo oss på wäg till den 1/4 mil aflägsna "Gran", en obebodd holme af circa en fjerdedels mils omkrets, utan annan vegetation än några buskar samt ett och annat träd. — Kaptenen qwarstod wid styret ehuru hela aktern låg under wattnet. En wåg slungade honom dock slutligen derifrån uti hafwet. Strax derpå sjönk hela fartyget på circa 30 famnars djup, med sin till Sundswall destinerade, högst dyrbara laddning, knappt 3 timmars wäg från nämnde stad. De qwarwaran-

Websites mentioned in this chapter

News search engines

Ask.com News Search – http://news.ask.com

Bing News – www.bing.com/news

Google News – http://news.google.com

Highbeam Research – www.highbeam.com

NewsNow – www.newsnow.co.uk

Paperball – www.paperball.de

Rocketnews – www.rocketnews.com

Romso Nachrichten – www.romso.de

Topix – www.topix.com

Wikio – www.wikio.com

Yahoo! News – http://news.yahoo.com

Directories of news websites

ABYZ News Links – www.abyznewslinks.com

IPL2 Newspapers & Magazines – www.ipl.org/div/news

Kidon Media-Link – www.kidon.com/media-link

NewsLink – www.newslink.org

The PaperBoy – www.thepaperboy.com

Lists of newspaper archives on the web

ICON Newspaper digitization projects – http://icon.crl.edu/digitization.htm

US News Archives on the Web – www.ibiblio.org/slanews/internet/archives.html

Wikipedia List of online newspaper archives – http://en.wikipedia.org/wiki/List_of_online_newspaper_archives

Broadcast news

ABC News – http://abcnews.go.com

ARD – www.ard.de

BBC News – http://news.bbc.co.uk

CBC Archives – http://archives.cbc.ca

CBS News – www.cbsnews.com

CNN – www.cnn.com

FOX News – www.foxnews.com

MSNBC – www.msnbc.msn.com

ZDF – www.zdf.de

News agencies

Agence France-Press – www.afp.com/afpcom/en

Al Jazeera – http://english.aljazeera.net

Associated Press – www.ap.org

China View Xinhuanet – www.chinaview.cn/china/index.htm

Deutsche Presse-Agentur – www.dpa.de

Indymedia – www.indymedia.org

Inter Press Service – http://ipsnews.net

Interfax – www.interfax.com

ITAR-TASS – www.itar-tass.com/eng

Kyodo News – http://home.kyodo.co.jp

Reuters – www.reuters.com

United Press International – www.upi.com

Yonhap News Agency – http://english.yonhapnews.co.kr

Press releases

Asia Business News – www.abnnewswire.net

Business Wire – www.businesswire.com

Categorynet – www.categorynet.com

Hugin Online – www.hugingroup.com

Japan Corporate News Network – www.japancorp.net

Korea NewsWire – www.koreanewswire.co.kr

Marketwire – www.marketwire.com

PR Newswire – www.prnewswire.com

Presseportal – www.presseportal.de

PRWeb – www.prweb.com

Science news

AlphaGalileo – www.alphagalileo.org

EurekAlert – www.eurekalert.org

Informationsdienst Wissenschaft – http://idw-online.de/en

New Scientist – www.newscientist.com

Newswise – www.newswise.com

ScienceDaily – www.sciencedaily.com

ScienceNews – www.sciencenews.org

Historical newspaper collections

Die Digitale Bibliothek, Staatsbibliothek zu Berlin – http://
digital-b.staatsbibliothek-berlin.de/digitale_bibliothek/
digital.php?gruppe=zeitung

Digitized Swedish Newspapers – http://magasin.kb.se:8080/
searchinterface

Gallica La presse quotidienne – http://gallica.bnf.fr/html/
presentationPeriodiques.html

Hemeroteca Digital, Biblioteca Nacional de España – www.
bne.es/es/Catalogos/HemerotecaDigital

Historical Newspaper Library of Finland – http://digi.lib.helsinki.
fi/sanomalehti/secure/main.html?language=en

Irish Newspaper Archive – www.irishnewsarchive.com

NLA Australian Newspapers – http://newspapers.nla.gov.
au/ndp/del/home

Papers Past – http://paperspast.natlib.govt.nz/cgi-bin/paperspast

UK Gazettes – www.gazettes-online.co.uk

Discontinued news search engines in the Internet Archive

Internet Archive Wayback Machine – http://web.archive.org/
web/web.php. This is a good start page with information on
the search engine and the contents of the archive itself.

Excite NewsTracker – http://web.archive.org/web/*/http://nt.
excite.com

InfoSeek News Channel – http://web.archive.org/web/1998*/
http://www3.infoseek.com/Topic?tid=1486

Net2One – http://web.archive.org/web/*/www.net2one.com

3

Professional news search services

Abstract: The professional fee-based news search services provide a number of advantages over the free news search engines, among them advanced search features, greater depth and scope of coverage, and access to back archives. The major services include Factiva, LexisNexis and DIALOG, all of which offer advanced searching techniques such as Boolean and proximity operators, specialized syntax and truncation. The fee-based services index their articles manually, using controlled vocabularies and subject codes. Searching on parameters such as date, news source and language are reliable. Results can be obtained in a variety of formats. The fee-based services also offer saved searches and regular search alerts.

Key words: fee-based news search, online news search.

Introduction

While some of the free news search engines provide good coverage of many important news sources these tools do have their shortcomings. They will normally only let you search for articles published on the web during the past month; their support for more than the most basic search syntax is very limited; they lack professional and consistent indexing; and they generally don't index printed versions of newspapers. If these features are vital to your information needs, then you should consider using a professional news search service.

This chapter provides an introduction to the use of fee-based professional news search services, including **Factiva**, **LexisNexis** and **DIALOG**. It outlines the advantages of professional tools, such as advanced search features; stability of search syntax; width and depth of coverage; back archives; and permanence of access. It also provides a detailed description of advanced search techniques. These include using Boolean and proximity operators, wild cards, truncation and parentheses and making good use of index terms. Professional news search services also offer saved searches and search alerts and can thus be used as an alternative to news and media monitoring services.

Advantages of professional search services

Professional online search services existed for years before the World Wide Web became popular in the early 1990s. They provide exceptional search tools, but at a considerable cost. Learning to master difficult search syntax used to be of the utmost importance so as to keep costs to a minimum, and training was therefore essential. Some of the best of these search services are the so-called Big Three: DIALOG, (which is now owned by ProQuest), LexisNexis and DowJones Factiva. These premier online search services have been around for a very long time.

The initial version of the DIALOG search system was functional as early as 1966. The legal search provider LEXIS started in 1973 and launched its news search database, NEXIS, in 1979. The youngest of the three started out as Dow Jones Reuters Business Interactive but was rebranded as Factiva and has operated under that name since 1999. Professional news searching is just one of the many things that these services provide. To this day the Big Three remain the most popular because of the amazing breadth and depth of their scope and coverage. DIALOG was actively involved in the creation of online search services in the 1960s and today offers access to over 900 databases.

These services use several different pricing schemes and you will have to do some serious thinking about what will benefit you most among the available choices. If you work in a major company or organization with interests in the media there may already be access to a service like these. As an individual, your best option is generally to use transaction-based pricing as opposed to flat-fee deals. The latter will probably be too expensive anyway if you don't have your own business providing search services and business intelligence. For instance, the comparatively young Factiva service has a model where you pay a relatively inexpensive annual fee and then pay only for the full text of articles. Searching is free once the annual fee is paid, which means that you can practise searching all you want and learn without worrying about costs. Depending on which country you reside in, your billing options may vary.

One of the great things about professional search services is that when they use a pricing scheme that includes free searching you can always try to find the articles themselves on the free web. It can be a bit time consuming, but this way you can actually save a lot of money. Enter the title of an article you wish to read as a phrase search in your favourite web search engine – you will be surprised at how many articles you will be able to retrieve this way. This is particularly true for very recent news articles. In other cases, accessing articles at an additional cost from within the search service may be a better choice. It all depends how much time you have and what you intend to do with the articles you retrieve. Immediate access and consistency of output format are advantages that you may need in certain situations.

All the advanced search features you need

Fee-based services have always had an abundance of advanced search features that enable users to tweak their searches in many interesting ways. However, it is only with the advent of the web and quite recently that they have become more user friendly. It takes a certain personality and much perseverance to master the intricacies of the older command search syntax. Fortunately, a lot of the most common and powerful search features can nowadays be used from within a web interface, using advanced search forms. The trickier stuff, however, is still most readily accomplished with the more arcane search logic involving the use of operators, wild cards and parentheses.

Stability of search syntax and features

One of the most annoying things about web search engines is their inherent instability. Search features tend to come and go and search syntax can be changed without warning. Interesting new search engines offering new approaches will typically be taken over by one of the big giants, and when this happens they can be taken off the web altogether. On the other hand, their search technology can, to some degree, become integrated into the buying company's own search engine. Many times, however, the reason for the takeover is simply to put a stop to the competition before it becomes a problem. Once this has been accomplished, the development of the search technology from the acquired company may be abandoned.

As a user you frequently find yourself using a new, powerful and innovative search engine, learning its strengths and weaknesses, only to see it suddenly disappear from the web one day. This is something you can avoid by using the fee-based search systems. They are stable, reliable and their search features evolve incrementally, so your search skills can grow, uninterrupted by sudden changes.

Depth and scope of coverage, back archives and permanence of access

In web search engines you are normally not able to search printed versions of news articles or recent articles that were not published on the web. Using the professional services you can search both, and you will also get access to news articles that predate the web. Today several of the big newspapers, like the *New York Times*, *The Times* and *Die Zeit* have digitized large amounts of their older output. In these cases they typically provide search tools that are based on optical character recognition and will let you read some articles for free, while you have to pay for others. In the fee-based systems, searching is not based on OCR processes, which means that the results of searching within article texts are always very accurate.

The crawler programs of the web search engines visit an unbelievable number of web pages every day and the size of their indexes exceeds several billion web pages. While this may lead you to think that they must surely find everything available on the web, this is in fact not the case at all. A large portion of the web, some say the largest by far, cannot be captured by the crawler programs of Google and the rest. Huge amounts of information remain in what is commonly referred to as the Invisible Web and cannot be found using the search engines.

The fee-based search services, on the other hand, primarily do not index web resources; rather, they index proprietary sources, which supply the material directly to their systems. The numbers of news sources found in these databases range from a couple of hundred to several tens of thousands. This may seem very little when compared to the number of websites that the search engines index, but the fact is that the coverage of the professional online services is much more complete within their field. The reason for this is that they offer near-complete coverage of all the most important source publications, with archives in some cases stretching back several decades.

If you want to find a press release that was issued through one of the news wires about the launch of some company at the beginning of the 1990s, then you will find it here. If you want to read the first news stories commenting on the 9/11 attacks in the US, you will also find them here. This is what you pay for – the knowledge that the information is there, somewhere, in the database and that it will stay there, that you can find it and you will be able to find it again if you lose it. It won't go away just because a company goes bankrupt or is bought up by a competitor that then removes all the information on the original company from the web.

However, there are gaps in the coverage, which is why we used the phrase 'near complete coverage'. Most importantly, there are all the articles by freelance writers that were removed from these databases as a result of the case *New York Times* vs. *Tasini* before the U.S. Supreme Court in

2001. Jonathan Tasini was the President of the US National Writers Union. The court ruled that newspapers may not license electronic copies of articles written by freelance journalists to online news databases without first securing permission from the authors or offering economic compensation.

This quickly led to the removal of a great many articles from the online services and is the reason why this kind of material, unfortunately, cannot to be found on them. There may be other omissions, such as the non-inclusion of very short articles. The bottom line is that the coverage, while exceptional, is not complete. You may sometimes have to go to a library and read articles on microfilm – not an altogether unpleasant experience if you have the time, but if you don't have the time it can be a major obstacle.

Indexing of articles

One of the crucial differences between web search engines and fee-based services is that the latter index news articles very thoroughly. There is often consistency of indexing across multiple sources and sometimes even across different databases. So what are the benefits of indexing and how does it compare to the usual free-text searching that we all use on a daily basis in the web search engines?

Indexing is all about adding value to the text and it is another of the things you pay for when using a professional service. For a properly indexed article not only will the text itself be searchable, but there will also be keywords, subject codes, individual searching of different sections of the articles, accurate information about time of publication, data from bylines, adequate geographical searching and much more.

Advanced searching techniques

The Boolean operators

We'll start with search syntax and Boolean operators. It's essential to know how the search service you're using treats searches with more than one word. The most common default behaviour of web search engines is to imply the operator AND between words. Your search results will therefore normally contain all the words that you entered, but in no particular order. In most hits the words will be widely separated.

Searching in commercial services, on the other hand, can behave differently. In some services entering several words one after another can mean that you are searching for an exact phrase, while in other services you have to use quotation marks around a phrase. When using an advanced search form, look for a search box where you can enter 'all of these words' rather than 'this exact phrase', if you want to use a simple AND between words.

The OR operator is especially useful with words or names that are difficult to spell or that have variant spellings. The first name of the composer Kaikoshru Sorabji is not easy to get right. For example, a search in one of the commercial news search engines generates hits with at least four different spellings. Another useful application of the OR operator is when several different words or terms have a similar meaning or can be used to express the same concept. By using them with the OR operator you can avoid missing interesting articles just because their authors have used a synonym of the word that you expected to find in the text. It's always useful to have a synonym dictionary to hand; you can also use one of the many synonym dictionaries on the web.

With the OR operator you can also construct search expressions that will retrieve different spellings of the same word. For example, there are many words that can be spelled either with the ending -ise (in UK English) or with -ize (in both UK and US English). There are also spelling variations such as colour/color or behaviour/behavior to take into account. You may be tempted to try solving some of these problems by using wild cards, but these can generate other words that you didn't foresee. In advanced search forms there is frequently a search box where you can search for 'at least one of these words', which is the same as using the OR operator. You should note that in LexisNexis you automatically get search results for both UK and US English, regardless of which spelling you use.

One of the more tedious aspects of information retrieval is wading through large numbers of uninteresting search hits. To deal with this, one of the most powerful operators that you can use is the sometimes overlooked NOT. You'll be amazed by how much more focused a search expression can become with a clever application of the NOT operator. Many words have more than one meaning and some also have several nuances, depending on how they're used. The trick is to find the words that are especially frequent in the linguistic contexts of the search results that are of no interest to you. Find the words that delineate the wrong contexts and then use the NOT operator to weed out those results. Try grouping them within a parenthesis using OR, and then putting a NOT in front of the parenthesis, like this: jazz NOT (coltrane OR mingus OR ayler).

When you use parentheses always consult the help pages to ascertain how powerful the operators are in relation to each other. A common feature of many search systems is that AND is always processed before OR. However, in some systems, like LexisNexis, it is the other way around, OR being processed before AND. You will need to consult your search service's documentation in order to learn the correct order of precedence among operators for that service.

Figure 3.1 Grouping different spelling variants separated by OR in a nested parenthesis in Factiva

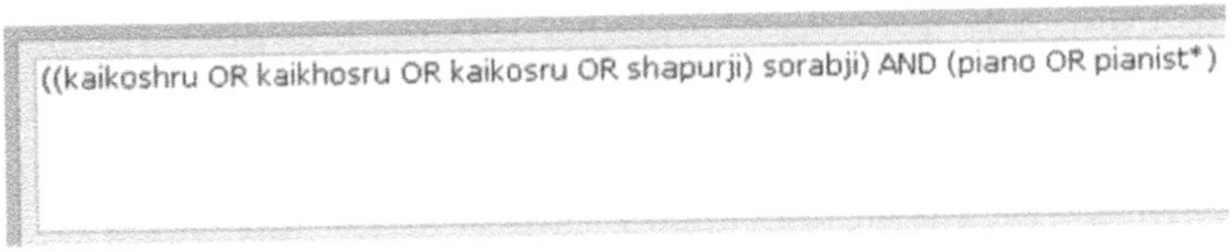

((kaikoshru OR kaikhosru OR kaikosru OR shapurji) sorabji) AND (piano OR pianist*)

Always group expressions with different spelling variants within parentheses and separate them by OR – otherwise the search expression may not work in the way you wanted. In most cases a NOT operator is more dominant than AND, but why take any chances? By using parentheses not only will you ensure that your search expressions are interpreted exactly as you intended, but also you yourself will understand them more easily. Sometimes you should consider using nested parentheses (Figure 3.1). In that case you will need to consult the help pages of the search service in order to find out how nested parentheses are supported and how different operators behave within them.

Using proximity operators and connectors

Proximity searching is one of the most important and powerful features of any search system. The most fundamental proximity search of all is the one used to delineate phrases. As we mentioned previously, web search engines like Google use quotation marks around the words that constitute the phrase. In Factiva you don't have to do this, and the search system automatically concludes that you are searching for a phrase when you enter several consecutive words. However, the most common syntax in professional search services is to use quotation marks around phrases. When searching for phrases you need to be aware of which words are used as operators by the search system; you may not be able to include such words in the phrase without first consulting the help pages. In most cases there will be a way to inactivate the operator function of the word, but exactly how this is done can vary from one system to another.

A phrase search is a special kind of proximity search where you specify which words you want to appear next to each other and their precise order. A less restrictive search can be done using an adjacency operator, of which one common type is ADJ. The ADJ operator is normally followed by a number that limits how many words can appear between the two search terms. With this operator the search words always have to come in the same order in the text as they are entered in the search expression. So: McEnroe ADJ9 Borg would mean that McEnroe has to appear before Borg and that there can be no more than eight words between McEnroe and Borg. This operator should only be used when you are certain that it is important for the words to appear in that order – to use it with McEnroe and Borg is probably not such a good idea!

In the example of the legendary tennis players McEnroe and Borg it's fairly obvious that it would be sufficient for the search that the names be near to each other in the text. This is where a proximity operator such as NEAR comes in handy. With this kind of operator you merely specify that the terms should appear within a certain number of words of each other, but not in any particular order. To find articles that mention both McEnroe and Borg in the same passage of text, use the NEAR operator combined with an appropriate number. In selecting the number of words that can occur in between it's wise not to be too restrictive, but not too generous either – 5 can be too few, whereas 25 may be too many, depending on the subject of the search.

Another kind of syntax that's frequently used in proximity searching is the letter W followed by a slash and a number representing the maximum word distance. Depending on the search system, this can mean either that the search words connected by the W operator must be in that particular order (Factiva and DIALOG) or that they can appear in any order (LexisNexis). To decide the order of words LexisNexis has the additional syntax, PRE/n, which enables you to specify the maximum number words between the search words while maintaining the order of the words in the search results.

In Factiva it's possible to specify that the search terms should appear within the same paragraph. This can be very useful as a way to avoid situations where your search terms, while appearing within a certain proximity to each other, are actually in different paragraphs, and therefore quite possibly located in different contexts. In LexisNexis you can do this by using its special within-paragraph operator, W/p. In LexisNexis's search system there are also operators for within sentence, W/s, and within segment, W/seg, adding even more flexibility. LexisNexis also supports using these 'within' operators preceded by the NOT operator. In this way you can exclude the search term in the second part of the search expression, as in Borg NOT W/p McEnroe. This can be a particularly powerful feature if you want to find paragraphs containing a particular word but not if some other word is also present. When you use proximity operators in conjunction with Boolean operators you will need to know the order of precedence in which all the different operators are handled by the search engine. You can assume nothing, especially if you use several different search systems.

Using wild cards and truncation

Another of the most powerful tools available to users of professional search systems is wild cards and truncation. (A wild card character is a character that can match any other character in a computer file.) This was actually a common feature in early web search engines such as AltaVista, but for some reason it is very rarely found in today's web search engines. In professional search systems you will always be able to use wild cards and truncation, and frequently in many different ways.

The most basic of all is right truncation. To right-truncate a word means to chop it off at a certain character boundary and allow the word to continue with any number of characters (bear in mind that one of these numbers is zero). This is usually called unlimited truncation. A typical example is 'research*' which tells the search system that matching words have to start with 'research' but can have any ending or no ending at all beyond the letter 'h'. In this example the truncation mark is an asterisk. This will work in Factiva, but other characters may be used, such as the exclamation mark in LexisNexis and the question mark in DIALOG.

A minimum number of characters must always be present before the truncation mark – it may vary, but it's normally three. The reason for this is that otherwise the search query would be too computationally demanding for the search engine – and probably not very useful anyway. In some cases you'll be able to use truncation that can be quantified. In Factiva, for instance, there's a syntax where you can use a dollar sign followed by a number to represent exactly how many additional characters you want to allow for. In other systems this is accomplished by using several asterisks, one for each additional character allowed (LexisNexis). This feature is called multiple character truncation and is much more restrictive in comparison to unlimited truncation.

Multiple character truncation can be useful in special cases but needs to be used sparingly, and not without a thorough analysis of the possible endings that may be of interest. The chances are that it will be too restrictive for most searches.

Please note in this context that the DIALOG search system uses question marks in a special way. One question mark at the end of a word means any number of characters; a question mark followed by a white-space and an additional question mark means a maximum of one additional character; while several question marks in a row means exactly that number of additional characters. These three variations are the means by which DIALOG implements unlimited, single-character and multiple-character truncation.

Right-truncation to allow for different word endings isn't the only way to use wild cards and truncation. There may be another wild card meta-character that you can use to represent exactly one character within a word. Once again, which character it is will vary, depending on the search service you use. The feature is frequently referred to as internal truncation or masking. An instructive and often-cited example is 'wom?n', with which you can search for 'woman' and 'women' at the same time. However, do be careful, because you can accidentally include irrelevant words in the search. Using expressions such as 'maximi?e' or 'globali?ation', you should be relatively safe. LexisNexis uses asterisks as wild cards within words, and you can use several in a row. Internal truncation is very useful in cases where different spellings of difficult names may appear in the text.

Finally, there are wild cards that can be used within phrase searches. Incidentally, this specialized application of wild cards is the only one supported by the leading web search engine Google. In Factiva you can use the per cent sign, '%', within a phrase to allow a word in a specific position to be any word. In this case it's important to remember that the per cent sign means exactly one word.

Some search systems automatically search for both the singular and the plural forms of a search word, whereas others take what you write literally. In LexisNexis you have to use special syntax to deactivate automatic simultaneous searching for both noun forms. Word searches in LexisNexis even include possessive endings by default. This is a good thing, considering that you would normally be interested in such search results as well. However, in some situations the default behaviour may not be desirable. For this reason LexisNexis provides syntax by which you can search explicitly for singular or plural noun forms.

Before leaving the topic of truncation we should mention that sometimes the expression 'word stemming' is used in the context of truncation. This isn't entirely correct because stemming is something much more complicated and specific than mere truncation. Search engines with true support for word stemming have a linguistic awareness of all the different words that are related to a single word stem. This means that you can search not only for words that use the stem in its normal form but also for others that originate from the same word stem but appear in an altered form.

Examples of this are irregular verb forms and plural forms other than the -s ending. Stemming can influence search results considerably, but to a varying degree, depending on the language of the search. Research has established that English is not one of the languages where word stemming is the most efficient. In an experiment conducted by Stephen Tomlinson at Hummingbird Ltd the precision of the search was increased by 2 per cent for English. This can be compared to, for example, German (27 per cent) or Finnish (69 per cent). At any rate, true stemming is rarely seen other than in very specialized search engines.

Reserved characters and non-searchable characters

In all search systems there will be a few characters that will cause problems when included in a search query. Some characters will have special functions as reserved meta-characters. This means that the search system will not interpret them literally. An asterisk or a question mark may be a truncation mark, for instance. In some services there will be a way to make the system interpret such characters literally; in others there will not be, and these characters may even produce error messages. In Factiva reserved characters should either be omitted or appear in search expressions within quotation marks, otherwise you will get an error.

There will be characters that the search system won't let you search for in any way at all. These are called non-searchable characters and most systems have a few. Typical characters that tend to be non-searchable are full stops (periods), commas, slashes, hyphens and apostrophes. A non-searchable character is translated into white-space, so search expressions such as 'pepsi-cola' and 'pepsi cola' will be processed in the same way. Of course it would be convenient if one could search for all characters, but let's consider the hyphen for a moment. There are many words that are combinations of two words where some use a hyphen between the words whereas others don't. The same writer may even use both variants in the same text! Words such as white-space can even appear in three forms: white-space, whitespace and white space.

The fact that apostrophes are often non-searchable characters and are converted to white-space before being interpreted by the search engine can be a problem. The most important thing here is to realize that in expressions like 'Andrew's cat' you actually get a three-word phrase after the white-space has been inserted. This means that using some sort of truncation after the 'w' in Andrew won't work. You will have to use phrase searches such as 'Andrew's cat' or 'Andrew s cat' in such cases.

Case-sensitive search

Not many search engines have the ability to differentiate between upper and lower case letters. This is really only useful in very specific situations, when it can then be of crucial importance. In LexisNexis you have the syntax words NOCAPS and ALLCAPS that enable you to search for words with no capital letters or with capital letters only. Using the CAPS syntax, on the other hand, you specify that there should be *at least* one capital letter within the word. This typically matches the first letter of a name or the first word of a sentence. You should remember that the letters of indexing terms are often capitalized – so when you use ALLCAPS don't search in such a way that the syntax applies to indexing terms.

Combining the SINGULAR syntax with the ALLCAPS syntax in LexisNexis will solve some difficult problems if you use a complex nested expression like ALLCAPS (SINGULAR(abba)). This example will help if you want to retrieve articles mentioning the famous Swedish pop group ABBA. Powerful as these commands are, there are still special cases that can't be covered by them. Consider the classic computer hardware called NeXT. In this instance you won't be helped even by the CAPS syntax because it will retrieve all occurrences of the word 'next' at the beginning of a sentence. (Some readers may recall that early versions of the AltaVista web search engine were in fact able to handle the NeXT problem correctly.) Case-sensitive search is currently not implemented in DIALOG and Factiva.

Using field tags and advanced search forms

Usually there are a number of field tags or suffixes that you can use to accomplish more specialized searches. Look for a list of the ones that can be used in a normal search box. You will have to check how field tags behave in connection to operators because there may be some restrictions. Another means of doing more specialized searches is via an advanced search form with drop-down lists or radio-buttons, which enable you to select restrictions in a more convenient way. This can sometimes work against you because the people who construct search forms can't accommodate or predict all the features you might want to use. We recommend that you learn all the syntax that can be entered manually in the search boxes, even though this can be tedious and time consuming.

Searching headlines, lead paragraphs and article authors

Searching in the headlines of articles is a simple but effective way to make a search more focused. When writing a headline the author must come up with something that catches the attention of the modern reader, which isn't very easy. Many headlines are therefore very catchy but not necessarily very descriptive. This means that you shouldn't restrict yourself solely to headline searching if free text searching tends to generate too much information noise. If your search word is an uncommon one, searching in the full text of articles, as when using a web search engine, will be no problem. In other cases it won't work very well at all and you'll have to try to find a search query that generates a manageable number of results while not being too restrictive.

You should take advantage of the possibility of searching the first or lead paragraph. The topics that are most important in the article are always mentioned in the lead paragraph. Headlines and lead paragraphs can usually be searched either separately or in combination – the latter is probably the most effective choice (Figure 3.2). In rare cases there may also be document sections called highlights, which are brief descriptions mentioning key topics. If your search service has these highlights they can be searched too, which will add even greater precision. Other features that may be searchable include column names, section names, editions and corrections.

You won't be able to search very accurately for the author names of news stories when using general web search engines or news search engines. You can use a search expression like 'by Henry James', and it will work some of the time. Even though a few of the web search engines try to index the names of the authors of articles automatically there will always be errors. In the fee-based services, on the other hand, you can always search for article authors and get accurate results because authors' names are properly indexed. The author information is normally stored in a byline that is sometimes expanded to contain some biographical data.

Figure 3.2   Narrowing the focus by searching in headline and lead paragraph in Factiva

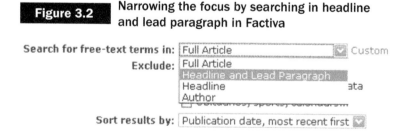

Using subject headings, index terms and content types

As stated before, one of the main advantages of using the professional search services is the fact that their databases are indexed in a consistent and professional manner. While web search engines lack this kind of indexing, some of them do try to extract concepts and keywords by using clustering technology. However, although they are sometimes useful these procedures can produce unpredictable and occasionally wildly incorrect results. They are also language specific and cannot be applied to search results in languages for which they are not intended.

The fee-based services manually index every article so as to provide the best possible subject codes and keywords, which are typically applied consistently to sources in many different languages. By taking advantage of this indexing you can perform very powerful searches, and again, there is nothing comparable in web search engines.

You will be using controlled vocabularies, as when searching for medical literature with MeSH terms. There will be a finely tuned system of subject codes and industry codes and it will probably be hierarchical. You can use the look-up feature to browse through the available codes and subjects in the search system and in this way you can find the most appropriate ones for your search (Figure 3.3). Professional manual indexing has been used for a long time in these databases and you should be able to find out when different subject codes and other terms were introduced.

Indexing adds another dimension to searching, and using index terms and codes is one of the best ways of adding precision to a search. In addition to using subject codes you may be able to restrict your search to one or more industries (for example using NAICS codes), countries or geographical

Figure 3.3 The interface for adding index terms to a search in LexisNexis

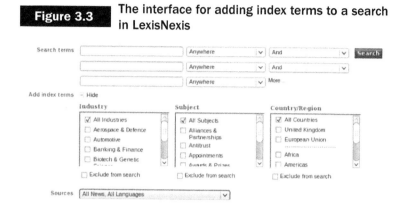

regions (Figure 3.4). You can combine all of these to further focus your search. Combining them with free text searching or searching in sections such as headlines and lead paragraphs can solve difficult search situations, such as when your search terms are ambiguous in some way.

Figure 3.4 Results grouped according to different indexes in the Discovery Pane in Factiva

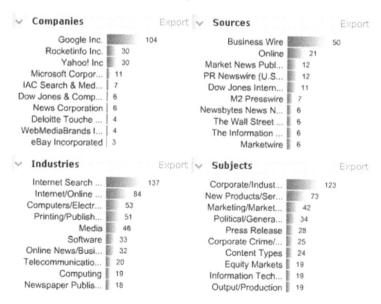

In web search engines you normally have to try to focus ambiguous words in other ways. You can try to do this by using search expressions that exclude terms that occur in contexts typical of a wrong interpretation of your search word. With controlled indexing you can avoid this tiresome task, which relies on your linguistic imagination and ability to find which terms to exclude. Not everything will be as straightforward as 'salsa NOT dance' when you're hungry for some hot food!

There may also be a few content types by which you can restrict your search. These can include interviews, obituaries, editorials, press releases, letters and profiles of persons and countries. Others can be news agency stories, commentaries and opinions, reviews and news transcripts. In some search systems these content types can be defined as subjects and will be found in the subject listings.

Word count operators and minimum number of mentions operators

If you want to avoid shorter articles and find more in-depth material, consider using a word count operator if your search service has one. With this kind of operator you can specify that matching articles must contain, for instance, 500 words or more and you will know that there won't be any shorter and possibly less informative articles among the results. A similar kind of search, and useful in focusing your search, is to specify a minimum number of occurrences for a search term. In Factiva and LexisNexis, for example, you can use the atleast*n* operator where *n* is the minimum number of mentions of the search word in the articles in your results list. There may also be drop-down choices, such as major mentions or three or more mentions, which make this kind of searching easier.

Date restrictions

Restricting searches by date ranges is something that's not really possible using web search engines such as Google. This is because it's difficult or impossible for the search engine to know the publication date of a normal web page. Dates on web pages either can't generally be trusted or are often missing altogether. In the fee-based commercial search systems this problem doesn't exist because the news articles in their databases are indexed manually and mostly relate to printed publications where a correct date can easily be determined.

How date ranges are specified can vary according to the search service and what search form you use. Some use graphical solutions where you pick dates from calendars, while in others you may have to use special syntax. Depending on your search needs, it can be very convenient to be able to use date restrictions – and to be confident that they will actually work.

Selecting source publications

Being able to restrict your search to certain source publications is of course great if you're looking for articles from specific sources. Otherwise, it's better to avoid it, as it can easily have a negative effect on your search results. Even if you feel convinced that only a particular set of sources could possibly contain articles of interest to you, there's always a chance that some new source has appeared or that another source has started publishing stories in your field of interest. You wouldn't want to miss those.

Publication types that you can expect to find are major newspapers, regional newspapers, international, regional and national newswires, business publications and wires, press releases, news transcripts, newsletters, some journals, magazines, a few scientific publications, statistics, industry-specific press and more. You should check that all the most important source publications are available from the search service to which you are planning to subscribe. Also, don't forget to take a look at what web-based news sources are indexed and to check whether they include some quality blogs. LexisNexis, for example, uses Newstex Blogs on Demand, which is generally considered to be a good blog source.

Searching on language

Limiting your search to languages that you can actually read is, naturally, recommended. It will help you to get a better overview of search results, as well. You can be confident that the article language has been indexed correctly, because in professional search services the indexing is not based on automatic language detection. Even though this technology is a powerful tool that works most of the time, it's not entirely foolproof in your normal web search engine, as you will probably have noticed.

Sometimes you may want to find stories in languages that you don't read. If this is very important, as in business intelligence, you can get a manual translation by paying for it. For limited text segments, rough translations can be done by search engines that offer automatic machine translation for free. You can use this first to help you decide whether it's worth the money to get a professional translation.

The quantity of sources from different countries and representing different publication types varies between the search services. An excellent coverage of English-language sources of high quality can be found in all of the Big Three. Their coverage of other languages varies considerably. If you need to search for news in French, German, Spanish, Italian and other European languages you need to look closely at the search service's source lists for the relevant languages. This applies even more so to non-European languages.

Search results

The results lists, sorting options and search within results

The default sorting in news searching is nearly always chronological, with the newest articles first. The option used by the search engine to sort by the relevance ranking can be an interesting one, and in rare cases it can be the default behaviour. Usually you will also have an option to sort your results in ascending chronological order, i.e. with the oldest articles first. This is the way to go if you want to follow the development of a news topic from the initial event, the first commentaries and reactions and onwards. You need to be aware that there will probably be a way to search within your search results. This can be very handy if you get interesting results but not all of them with a focus on the aspects that you're interested in.

You'll probably be able to use various options to customize the results views to your own liking. One thing that you should consider is something that can be available during searching, which is the use of duplicate detection (Figure 3.5). If this feature is available in your search system, you can get a less cluttered and less repetitive results list. How well the duplicate detection works and whether it can be configured varies between systems. You will have to experiment and you may find that it works to your advantage in some cases. While browsing through the results you

Figure 3.5 Applying varying degrees of duplicate detection in Factiva

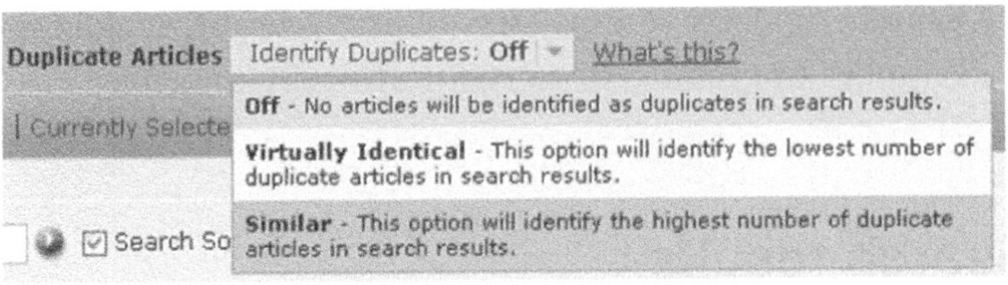

may be able to tag documents for viewing at a later stage. There may even be versioning support within the results views, which means that different versions of the same article can be marked as such, using an icon or some textual indication.

The results views normally include headline, source publication and metadata such as author, source, date and word count. This is frequently the basic list format offered; typically there are also extended list views that include the beginning of the lead paragraph or snippets from the article text that show the search words in context. Instead of using a list view you may also be able to browse the articles one by one, using different formats. Normally there is a full-text format that includes just the basic metadata. Additionally there will be full-text formats that include the full range of indexing terms assigned to the article. A special format is viewing only keyword-in-context extracts from the text. Finally, there may be an option to create your own output format by selecting the various fields that you want to see, as in LexisNexis.

It's not uncommon to have a section alongside the search results where they're arranged in groups according to various criteria. This is increasingly frequent practice in many search systems, and even in web search engines. In the fee-based services where there are many index terms from different data fields these groupings can be very useful. It's much more difficult for web search engines to provide really useful groupings because there are no reliable metadata in your normal HTML. Here, the groups can include languages and geographical regions but, however frequently correct, they're actually educated guesses by computer programs. Another feature is the use of clustering technologies, which can yield lists of particularly prevalent keywords or concepts. While clustering invariably produces a few nonsensical groups, the more successful applications can give you valuable input in the form of related search terms or phrases.

Clustering of keywords and concepts may also occur within the search systems of the professional search services. Groupings that will typically appear in fee-based services include subjects and industries, according to the indexing. While these may provide some interesting filtering, those that use named entities such as source publications, companies and geographical regions provide even more focused options and indications. A list of companies can provide clear pointers as to which ones are doing business in areas related to your search. Lists of source publications will tell you which ones most frequently include articles on your topic of interest and they may lead you to conduct broader searches using specific source publications as a search filter. There can also be graphs indicating the time spans during which large numbers of articles matching your search query have appeared. The various groupings are typically clickable so that you can use them to quickly refine your search.

Output formats

As explained above, there may be other kinds of output than the full article to choose from. These include keyword in context (KWIC), headlines plus lead paragraphs and indexing, or full articles including all available indexing. Beware that there can be different price tags, depending on what you choose. You should check this beforehand so as to avoid getting any unpleasant surprises.

In addition to the formats that you can access within the search service there are other output formats for downloading, delivery or printing. These can include HTML, word processor formats like RTF or Microsoft Word, PDF and sometimes XML formats. You can expect these options to be clearly outlined, with the possibility of including all available metadata and indexing, according to what you choose. Mark-up of search words is very convenient and the online services normally provide it in these output formats. Mark-up may not be available in fixed output formats such as PDF files, but it's not really necessary, except possibly in very long articles, where it may be desirable for convenience' sake.

Search histories and saved searches

While trying out different search strategies and search expressions you often take one step forward and two steps backward, start over several times and only gradually start to find your way. Following your own steps and studying the progression from good to bad and from better to excellent is recommended for your development as a searcher. The tool to use for this is your search history, which will be displayed somewhere in the user interface and will enable you to return to a previous search that was the most successful of a whole batch you tried out.

In some services previous searches can be accessed as search sets that can be combined freely using Boolean logic, adding a new level of flexibility. Search histories are normally only retained on a session basis. This means that when you log out of the search system you won't be able to return to these search expressions. In LexisNexis, however, recent searches and a list of recently viewed documents are retained – for a period of one week for searches and 48 hours for documents. There is a limit of 100 items for each of these histories.

When you want to return to a search that you did some time ago is where the saved searches feature of some systems comes in handy. If saved searches are available you can store search expressions so that you can return to them and run them again. You can also use them as a starting point for further explorations in related search expressions.

In this way you can build search strategies incrementally across sessions, fine-tuning your search so as to retrieve increasingly relevant and precise results. During this process you should delete previous search expressions that you have saved but now find ineffective, retaining only the really good ones. You'll probably need to give your search expressions names, which will be displayed when you browse your saved searches. Keep them simple and descriptive.

Search alerts

When you start to feel reasonably confident that you've found the most effective search expression for a certain information need you may find it tedious to run the same search manually session after session. Perhaps it's crucial for you to find any new results that your search expressions yield but you really don't have time to constantly rerun them. This is when you should consider taking the next step and letting the search system run it automatically at specified intervals.

This is called search alerts and is a very convenient way to handle your searching. It's seldom available free of charge, as in some of the free news search engines such as Google News or Yahoo! News. There will typically be a monthly fee on a per-search-expression basis for using search alerts. You'll have to consider the likely cost if you need to use several search alerts and decide whether they're sufficiently necessary for you to pay the price.

The most common delivery method for search alerts is by email. Before you start mail-bombing yourself, run the search manually for a period of time so as to study how often new articles appear that match your search criteria. If there seem to be too many new results within a short time span you may want to revise your search expression before using it in an alert. The quantity of incoming new articles will also influence your decision regarding how often the alerts should be delivered. Normally you have the option of having them delivered once a day or receiving them continually, as they become available.

If you decide to use a scheduled email delivery you will normally be allowed to specify a time of day. This can either be an hour of your choice or simply in the morning or the afternoon. In any case, don't forget to specify your time zone in the appropriate menu. Naturally, you should consider the time of day when you will be most likely be able to read your alerts and choose accordingly. In some cases you can get alerts at one, two or three different times in one day. It may also be possible to get your alerts from Monday to Friday, rather than from Monday to Sunday.

Getting daily digests is normally a good choice; but you may have good reasons for wanting to receive updates by continuous email alerting. This is something you should resort to only if time is so essential to your information needs that delays can be a source of vulnerability or inconvenience. If you frequently have to make urgent business decisions this is definitely the way to go. At the other end of the spectrum, there may be options for weekly or even monthly deliveries if your search yields very few results and time is not crucial.

There are other criteria besides the delivery interval that you need to decide upon when you create search alerts. One such may be the maximum number of search results, if you use search expressions that tend to yield many new results each day. Another thing to consider is whether you want to receive the results sorted by date and hour or by relevance. This won't matter if your search query will return only a few articles each day, but if the results are likely to be more than 10 (which may be the default number that is delivered) on each occasion you will probably need to specify that you want more than 10 results.

If you don't want to see more than 10 results anyway, an important question is how they are to be sorted. If this option is available you can choose between chronological or by relevance. Both choices have their downsides. If you choose chronological order you may miss articles that were published just after the time of day for your previous delivery (because, for example, if there are 25 new hits since your last delivery, you will see only the 10 most recent ones). If, on the other hand, you choose relevance, you will be at the mercy of the automated relevance algorithm that your search service uses.

The formatting of the alerts may be configurable, but it should at least include headlines and lead paragraphs, with links to the full text articles. Again, you may be able to use duplicate detection, applying a variable degree of similarity up to nearly identical. Choices for the format of the email message itself can be plain text, HTML or maybe a format appropriate for reading on a mobile device. The latter choice will be desirable if you do a lot of reading while on the go, outside the normal office environment.

You should definitely think carefully about which email address to receive your alerts at if you have several alerts, and most especially if you opt for continuous delivery. A separate email account for alerts can be a sensible solution and there are lots of free email services that you can use. Gmail.com, for instance, provides excellent search capabilities that can be incredibly time saving if you have numerous alerts. Getting your normal email box cluttered with search alerts can rapidly become a major problem!

Client billing

If you're an information professional offering search services to other parties, you should look for client billing tools. A very practical feature that is often available in fee-based systems is the possibility to assign account names (Factiva) or project IDs (LexisNexis). These are great, because when you download documents you can mark the expenses for different clients. This will save you a lot of time in sorting out what to bill to whom. Look for monthly break-downs according to different account names.

Other fee-based services

Newspaperarchive.com from Heritage Microfilm is by far the largest archive of historical newspapers on the internet. It offers access to many tens of millions of newspaper pages from 1759 onwards and will add another 25 million pages in 2010. Its content is mostly English language, with a heavy emphasis on newspapers from the US, Great Britain and Ireland. There are a few other newspapers from countries such as Japan, Denmark, Germany, South Africa, Jamaica and China, but only a small number. To be able to search, browse and view the scanned images you need to have a subscription. You can choose one month for $18 or sign up for a year, which will bring the monthly cost down to $10. There are sometimes introductory offers that are even cheaper. Newspaperarchive.com has a section called The Daily Perspective which is sort of a blog where members of its community share stories that they have found in the archive. Visitors can view the images accompanying the blog posts for a limited time without charge.

NewsLibrary.com, from NewsBank, is a vast archive containing some 182 million US newspaper articles. The most important newswires, and transcripts from broadcasting services can also be found there. This is not a place to find historical newspapers; on the contrary, the focus is on the present day and many of the sources have an archive that goes back only a few years. Searching is free in NewsLibrary.com, which makes it an excellent free news search engine for US content. It has a powerful search interface that will let you search in headlines, lead paragraphs, bylines, captions, index terms and the full text. Individual articles cost $2.95, while a monthly fee of $19.95 will buy you 25 articles.

Pressdisplay.com is like a huge online kiosk where you can read PDF versions of printed newspaper issues on the same day that they are published. Currently it offers more than 14,000 newspapers from over 80 countries. Using the Economy Subscription plan for $9.95 a month you can read 31 issues per month. The issues can be from the same newspaper or, if you like, you can change newspaper every day. For each additional issue that you want to read you have to pay one credit. With the Economy Subscription plan each credit is $0.75. You can also buy individual issues without a subscription, but in that case they cost $0.99 each. Pressdisplay.com has a powerful search engine that can be used without charge. You can search in individual news sources, set date limits, choose language, search for authors and search in headlines. Some of the older results that you get when you search will not be available for viewing because back issues are constantly being removed.

Several of the major US newspapers provide archive search and sell their older articles through **ProQuestArchiver** from ProQuest. The content in ProQuestArchiver is also searchable in Google News Archive Search. However, the search interface in ProQuestArchiver is better than Google's and offers more advanced features, such as truncation. If you don't have an account for one of the Big Three online services ProQuestArchiver offers a good alternative for the newspapers that have chosen to store their back archives here. The scanned historical articles from these newspapers are available only through ProQuestArchiver. They include dailies such as the *Washington Post, Los Angeles Times, USA Today, Chicago Tribune, New York Post* and *Boston Herald*. The back archives may cover their whole or nearly their whole publishing history, as for the *Chicago Tribune* (1852–), *Washington Post* (1877–) and *Los Angeles Times* (1881–). The pricing of articles varies; $3.95 for single articles is quite common.

Websites mentioned in this chapter

DIALOG – www.dialog.com

Dow Jones Factiva – www.factiva.com

LexisNexis – www.lexisnexis.com

NewsLibrary – http://newslibrary.com

NewspaperArchive – www.newspaperarchive.com

ProQuestArchiver – www.pqarchiver.com

PressDisplay – www.pressdisplay.com

4

News monitoring services

Abstract: News or media monitoring services deliver regular search results based on criteria supplied by the customer. They vary in quality and in their coverage of sources, and their searching techniques can sometimes produce a high proportion of irrelevant results. Careful evaluation is advisable before subscribing to a service.

Key words: media monitoring services, news monitoring services.

Introduction

There are a great many news monitoring services (NMS) available today, most of which charge a fee. They have grown in popularity and their marketing efforts have been aggressive. Some are of high quality and have been in the business for decades; many have followed the trend of monitoring free resources on the internet, particularly social media networks. A lot of the newcomers focus exclusively on social media. We won't name individual NMS much in this chapter because there are so many and it would have been too expensive and time consuming for us to test many of them. Instead, we will provide some general remarks and advice concerning how you should go about evaluating them.

Regardless of whether they are newcomers or established monitoring services, you should always question whether they really are worth the money. Don't let yourself be seduced by the salesman who offers the ultimate business intelligence service that will save you more time than any other similar service can. Always ask yourself: 'What can they do for me that I can't do myself if I just spend a little time to learn or attend a course on information retrieval?' You should always compare what they can do for you with what can be done using free tools or, if you are going to pay anyway, with what the professional search services such as those described in Chapter 3 enable you to do.

Describing news monitoring services

What exactly is an NMS and how is it different from free news search engines and commercial news databases? News monitoring services provide the customer with news and other content of interest, sometimes with documentation and analysis, delivered by email, regular post or even SMS. They are sometimes called media monitoring services because they may capture not only printed and online news but also news from TV and radio. Some other related names are media or press cutting services or agencies, media intelligence or information logistics services.

They can differ quite a lot, but they have one common feature, the marketing of themselves as the optimal business intelligence solution, offering companies exactly what they need so as to keep track of the surrounding world. Let's look at how some of these NMS explain their mission and what they do:

> Esmerk: ... aims to provide you each day with the business information you need to keep on top of your markets, your competitors and your business

environment – information to keep you ahead. Your daily Esmerk feed is tailored to your specific requirements, giving you only the information you need.

Cymfony: ... collects all forms of content, organizes and categorizes it, and provides a powerful but easy-to-use interface with data visualization and discovery features that allow you to gain valuable insights from selected discussions most relevant to your brand.

CustomScoop: ... customize each client account to deliver meaningful media intelligence to make our customers more effective and efficient. With a database that includes hundreds of thousands of newspapers, magazines, web sites, blogs, podcasts, and more, you can be confident in your results.

Cision keeps track of: ... what's being said about you on social media sites, print publications, TV/radio, and on the Internet. Get the latest coverage of your brand. No matter where in the world your story breaks. And share your coverage across the globe. Understanding where public perception is today so you can guide where it goes tomorrow.

Durrants helps you to: ... never miss any of your coverage with over 10,000 UK sources monitored continuously, from print to online to broadcast as well as coverage from 100 markets globally.

Cyberalert: ... local, national and worldwide press clipping, news monitoring, broadcast monitoring and social media monitoring services offer today's best media monitoring value: unequaled media coverage, extraordinarily accurate clipping, automated daily e-mail alerts containing all new media mentions found in the previous 24 hours ....

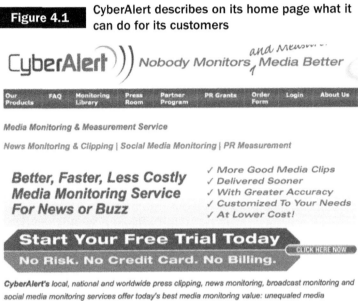

Figure 4.1 CyberAlert describes on its home page what it can do for its customers

A short history of news monitoring services

The forerunners of NMS appeared in the middle of the nineteenth century and were called press clipping agencies. In 1881 Henry Romeike in London started what has been called the world's first clipping service, aimed at artists wanting to read what was written about them in the news. The agency later became Romeike & Curtice and quickly expanded to New York, Berlin and Paris.[1] Other sources claim that Alfred Chérié was even earlier when he started a similar service in 1879, also tailored to the needs of artists wanting to keep track of their worldwide reputations and delivering reviews of their performances. Whole articles were rarely supplied, just the section or sentence that included their names.[2] Frank Burrelle and his wife, Nellie, started Burrelle's Press Clipping Bureau in New York in 1888 when Frank, working as an attorney, saw a demand for clipping services for businessmen.

In the twentieth century the invention of radio and television broadcasting made them the next target for monitoring, in addition to printed news and articles. When information retrieval technology and databases were developed in the 1960s and 1970s it became possible to find bibliographic information on articles using computers and many of the monitoring services began to take advantage of these technical developments. During the 1990s they also began to monitor news published on the web and today most monitoring services include web sources in one way or another. Some focus mainly on the web and what is said in news stories and social media networks about, for example, a company, an organization or an individual. Some monitoring services are focused primarily on following the buzz about brands and don't do other subject-related queries. This is especially common among the services that follow brands in the social media networks.

The meaning of news monitoring services

The term 'news monitoring service' is occasionally used in a very broad sense, thereby including, for instance, Google News with its email alert service. To us, monitoring services are services that scan a broad range of media sources on demand and deliver content either digitally by email or RSS feed or in hard copy by regular mail, according to the wishes of their customers. Google News scans web sources solely but can, in addition to being categorized as a free news search engine, also be categorized as an NMS because it has an email alert service. Alert services are closely related to what is sometimes referred to as SDI or selective dissemination of information. This concept comes from the field of library and information science and SDI became popular when literature databases evolved in the 1970s and 1980s, before the birth of the web. A so-called SDI profile is an automated search that is executed periodically and informs users about new items matching the search. The term SDI has become more or less obsolete and has been abandoned in favour of the term 'alert service'. However, the purpose remains the same, to push information on a regular basis about new items of interest. In the last few years many of the research databases that initially offered SDI services have started to offer RSS feeds as an alternative to email alerts.

Basic news search is not a particularly complicated task and doesn't take any more of your time than other types of search. However, if you want to perform a comprehensive search for a specific topic, using advanced search syntax and filtering, and in as many relevant sources as possible, it will take much more time. You have to learn about search refinements, which are the most suitable tools, and check which news sources they include. If you read Chapter 5 about evaluation of news search tools you will get a better understanding of many of the aspects you need to consider. You will discover, if you haven't already, that comprehensive and advanced news searching does indeed take a lot of time, practice and patience. This is exactly why many users with urgent information needs are willing to pay for an NMS that promises to do all the hard work for them. After all, time is money.

Unfortunately these services all too often fail to perform a comprehensive search in all the relevant sources. In the worst cases they will just scan free news sources on the web, applying simple keyword matching. They might offer ways to exclude words, but they seldom use subject indexes or any advanced search features, such as truncation. Sometimes they don't even index the monitored sources properly and the selection of news sources can be insufficient or of debatable quality.

Evaluating your monitoring service

The most important things to evaluate in NMS are:

- the specific sources and types of sources that are included
- how the NMS monitors these sources and how it delivers results.

As always with news search and monitoring tools, it's very important to find out which sources are included – particularly if you're going to be paying for it. Some will monitor only free news sources on the web, and if that's the case you need to be aware that you can monitor most of these news sources yourself using the free news search tools discussed in Chapter 2. The only valid reason why you should pay in this case is because the NMS delivers news articles of better relevance than those you are able to find using the free tools. You should also look at the selection of sources scanned by your monitoring service as compared to the free news search engines and, particularly, the professional news search services. The latter in most cases index many more high-quality web sources and they are frequently excellent at covering printed news.

Unfortunately, many of the monitoring services search for your topic using only simple word matching. This means that if you want to monitor and retrieve everything of value that is written, for instance, about Volkswagen cars you will merely get all news stories where the word Volkswagen is mentioned. In one of the stories a Volkswagen may have been involved in a car accident. Let's assume that this information is irrelevant to you. There may be many stories about car accidents that mention Volkswagen, thus producing many irrelevant results. You may use a search operator to exclude a word such as 'accident', but then you could miss a relevant article with a sentence like 'I bought my new Volkswagen by accident'.

It can be even worse when a word has several meanings. If the name of a brand that you want to monitor is one like Nike you will retrieve not only stories about shoes and clothes but also those mentioning the Greek goddess. There are also people who have Nike as their first name. You will have similar problems if you haven't identified important synonyms or abbreviations. In the Volkswagen case you may need to monitor the word VW as well. Cars can also have other names, such as the Volkswagen type 1, nicknamed the Beetle. You may even have to consider using the names of different Volkswagen models, like Polo or Golf. Monitoring the word Golf would obviously be a big problem because of its other common meanings. In the case of the car model Golf the easiest solution would be to also monitor for car-related words in the text. But anyone with some experience of information retrieval will know that there will probably be some car articles mentioning Volkswagen that also mention golf as a sport in a subordinate clause.

It's in situations like this that the problems of irrelevance in news search can become irritating and it's important to understand what the different monitoring services can do about it. You may think that they all use highly professional tools with advanced algorithms that will solve semantic problems such as the ones mentioned here, but that is probably too much to hope for. It's very common for any customized search alert that you set up to have to be fine-tuned more than once. In particularly difficult cases even that won't help. You should also realize that some NMS don't allow users to define the search alerts themselves. In those cases it's very hard to evaluate the service because you don't know how the search result has been extracted. They won't tell you how the query was formulated, what keywords were used and what search filters were applied.

Irrelevance in news monitoring services

There is a Swedish monitoring tool that attempts to discover real estate of interest by scanning a selection of relevant websites. Sometimes it confuses the name of a city with the first name of a real estate agent. Although it's not that common with names and places that have the same spelling, if you're unlucky you can end up with a high percentage of irrelevant records in your alerts. That can be very irritating. This is just one example of many, and if you think it's impossible for your topic to get confused with other topics, you can rest assured that one day you *will* get irrelevant records that will surprise you. Hopefully there will not be too many; and at least there's one good thing about irrelevant records – they will give you more insight into some of the most frequently occurring information retrieval problems.

What's most important is that the percentage of irrelevant hits is kept reasonably low and that you don't lose important items because of insufficient coverage of news sources or bad topic detection. It's not very easy to evaluate the abilities of monitoring services in connection to topic detection. Many of them will state that they use advanced linguistic techniques like NLP (natural language processing), or will try to hide things by using technical jargon. In most cases irrelevance is easy enough to discover, but it's much harder to find out about possibly relevant records that you may have missed. A well-known issue in information science is the fact that when you search with simple word matching you will quite often miss items that are on topic but don't mention the word you used. One strategy to avoid this is to set up several search alerts using different keywords to describe your topic. If you do this, however, there's a risk that you will also get more irrelevant records.

After evaluating your alerts you'll probably decide to delete some of them and fine-tune others. You may of course broaden a single search alert using the OR operator, but sometimes it's easier to evaluate alerts when they're separate. Again, all services will not allow you to work with the alerts directly in this manner. Each time you get an alert you should check how many irrelevant items you have received. If there are many, try to figure out what the problem is. If you get more than, say, 25 per cent of irrelevant records this can start to affect your ability to work effectively and you will probably need to reformulate your search alerts.

Another important way to evaluate your NMS is to use the tools that we've mentioned in other chapters in this book and see whether you can find items that your NMS hasn't found for you. For example, if you know that your monitoring service is scanning a certain website you could try to search using the internal search engine of the website or using a free news search engine. If you find other news stories using the same search query as in the search alert from your service, you should try to find out why your service didn't detect those stories. There can be several explanations, but it's not unusual for it to be the result of insufficient indexing by the monitoring service. In such a case you may want to reconsider whether your service is worth the money you're paying for it. That being said, news and media monitoring services can sometimes work perfectly well and be great tools saving much time for many customers with busy schedules of other things to attend to.

Sample list of news monitoring and related services

AAP Newscentre – www.newscentre.aap.com.au

BurrellesLuce – www.burrellesluce.com

CustomScoop – www.customscoop.com

CyberAlert – www.cyberalert.com

Durrants – www.durrants.co.uk

Ebiquity – www.ebiquity.com

Esmerk – www.esmerk.com

Jamedia – www.jamedia.com

Media Monitors – http://mediamonitorsgroup.com

Media Research Group – www.mrg.com.au

Meltwater – www.meltwater.com

NewsNow – www.newsnow.co.uk/services/

Retriever – www.retriever-info.com

Notes

1. *Encyclopedia of journalism*, ed. Christopher H. Sterling, Volume 1, London: Sage Reference, 2009.
2. *Art criticism and its institutions in nineteenth-century France*, ed. Michael R. Orwicz, Manchester: Manchester University Press, 1994, p. 174.

5

Evaluating news search tools

Abstract: A range of factors influence the efficacy of news search tools, including frequency of spidering source websites, the range and age of sources indexed and the quality and depth of indexing. Evaluation should include testing the advanced search features and the output and display options, and monitoring search results over a period of time. Other features to check are ease of customization, detection of duplicate articles and the availability of alerts or RSS feeds.

Key words: evaluation, news search tools.

Introduction

When you first start using a news search tool you'll probably have no inclination to evaluate it. If you plan to use a particular tool on a regular basis you may find it useful to take the time to read through this chapter. By following the advice concerning evaluation issues that we present here you'll also gain a deeper knowledge of how news search really works – or at least, how it should work. This is because many of the news search tools don't work in quite the way they're supposed to, in one or more respects. Of course, news search is similar to normal search in many respects, but there are also important issues to consider that are unique to news search. Here the aim is to stop searching uncritically, and not to settle for results that are merely 'good enough'.

Frequency of spidering

When using a web search engine, a good way to test the spidering frequency is to use the cached copy that's made available on several web search engines. (Spidering frequency refers to the frequency with which the search engine's crawler program visits websites for updates.) In Google the link to the cached copy can be found near the URL in the results lists. Click on it, and you will see a copy of the web page as it appeared the last time the spider visited it. You could say that a search engine index consists of asynchronous snapshots of the internet. The front pages of most news sources are typically updated several times every hour and of course it's difficult for the spiders to keep up with this. However, when evaluating news search engines you can't use the cached copy to determine how recently a page was captured because news search engines normally don't offer a cached copy. This means that you'll have to do your evaluation more or less manually. An interesting experiment can be done by watching a sports event on TV. Choose some really big event, like a high-profile soccer match of international significance. You don't have to watch the whole game, just the last part so that you know who won and maybe who scored the winning goal. Then, as soon as the match ends, go to your computer and start searching your favourite news search engines using keywords such as the names of the teams and of the player who scored the most crucial goal. Do the search every 15 minutes in two or three news search engines that you want to check up on. Note how many hits you get each time in each of the news search engines that are relevant to the just-finished match and cite the match score. Give it an hour, or maybe one and a half hours. The results will reflect how effective their spidering and indexing is.

Some news search engines may crawl the news sites very frequently, but perhaps not very deeply. By this we mean that while they may reindex the content of the home page and the start pages of major news sections, they don't go very deep each time they visit the websites. It's difficult to determine just how often a full reindexing of a source site is done. It could actually turn out to be very irregular. A test over a couple a days may give you a hint as to the typical spidering frequency.

It's important to check these things, so as to find out how fresh the search engine index normally is and whether this is good enough for your needs. In commercial news search databases this test won't be very helpful because they don't index web pages other than as a complement to the indexing of articles that they receive in other ways. Many but not all NMS provide you with news both from the internet and from the printed versions. There are lots of monitoring services around the world and some of them were established long before the internet became a popular publishing platform. Even here, it's important to try to check the updating frequency of both the printed news stories and the stories published on the websites that are being monitored.

Sources

How old is the archive?

Free news search engines on the internet typically index just the very latest news. It's not unusual for them to keep articles in the index for only 30 days. Reading the help pages should give you a hint as to how old the archive is. Another way to check is to use the advanced search form (if there is one) and see if it's possible to search by date. You may find some indication there, but even if they state that the database is 30 days old you may still need to do some tests. Generally, search engines tend to claim that they have lots of features, but they don't always live up to their ambitions.

For example, if they claim to index the major news sources going back 30 days that doesn't mean that they are indexing some of the more peripheral news sources in the same way. They seldom reveal this kind of information unless you ask for it specifically. If users would ask more often, do some evaluating of their own and require the news search engines to reveal their methods and live up to their goals it would be better for all users.

Take a news article that is 25–30 days old from one of the news sources that a news search engine claims to index, copy a sentence from it at random and paste it into the news search engine's search form. Use quotation marks at the beginning and end of the sentence. Maybe you will need to limit the search to this website as well. Try searching for the sentence to find out whether the article is indexed. Sometimes a news search engine can miss one or more articles, depending on different factors, even if its aim is to index the news source for 30 days back in time.

Most commercial news search services state very clearly which years of a certain news source they have indexed in their database. Nevertheless, random tests can sometimes be of interest even here, although these services are much less inconsistent than the free news search engines. You should also remember that it's not uncommon for some of the commercial services to index some news sources selectively. They generally inform users of any selective indexing in their help pages.

Types of sources indexed

It's not always easy to decide whether a website or publication is a news source or not. Some sources have both news stories and more in-depth articles that may or may not be news related. Some news search tools index both news and other news-related articles or postings. Besides regular news articles, they often include press releases, news agency stories and blog posts. It's important to check what types of sources news search engines index. Many newspapers have experimented in recent years with including blog posts in their own search results; some mark these clearly, while others don't. Many newspapers also have their own blogs, written by bloggers from their staff of journalists and freelancers and sometimes blog writers are recruited from the outside as guest writers because of their status as prominent persons or well-known bloggers.

News sources included

Finding a list of all the news sources included and how many there are is not always as straightforward as you may think. If you don't find one, you should ask for it. When you do get a list you should also check whether the news search engine really does index all of them by trying a random sample. Choose some of the most important sources and some of the more peripheral ones for your test.

If you use a particular search tool on a regular basis you'll be more aware of what sources it indexes; you can watch out while searching for any source that you remember but that isn't in the results lists. Of course it can depend on what subject you're searching for, but if you repeatedly get nothing from one particular source you should check again. Search engines, at least free news search engines, can change a lot from time to time, for different reasons. Always to keep a critical eye on your search tool is the best approach you can have as professional news searcher.

Languages and countries

Just because a news source is from a certain country, that doesn't mean it will use the language of that country, and vice versa. If you limit your search to the Swedish language you should also be able to find news stories published in Swedish-language newspapers in Finland, because Swedish is spoken by a minority in Finland and this group of people have their own newspapers, publishers, schools, theatres and much more. On the other hand, limiting to Finland should include both Finnish-language and Swedish-language newspapers in Finland, and maybe Sami newspapers in Finland. Another example is of a search engine indexing newspapers in France and in West Africa. Try searching for the name or some sentences from the actual content of a French-language newspaper from West Africa and limit the language to French. If you find something that is inconsistent you should email the search engine team. It's the only way to get the news search engines to work better.

Amount of indexing

Free news search engines don't always index whole articles, while sometimes they index too much, including irrelevant content. Many articles are taken from web pages that include content from other articles and in information boxes. Sometimes the search engine indexes this information too, and if the indexing algorithm isn't able to separate the content properly you will end up with irrelevant hits.

When you search for two or more words and find articles that are irrelevant, use the web browser's search function. The shortcut is nearly always Ctrl+F. Try to find each word that you searched for in the content of the page to see whether it exists in the article. If you don't find one of your words this can indicate, at least if you use Google News, that the word is not in the text itself but in a link-text pointing to that page.

As we already stated, sometimes news search engines don't index the full articles. Some index only the portion of the full text that's published in the RSS version. Choose one or two sentences from the end of the article to find out whether they have been indexed. If they've not been indexed, check some sentences from the beginning of the article. If that doesn't work either, try the heading from the top of the page. In some rare cases only the title has been indexed. This is probably because the search engine indexes RSS versions and only the headlines are included in the feeds from that source. This is not uncommon with news sources.

Inclusion of printed and/or web content

One of the most important and complicated problems with news sources within news search engines is the coverage. Traditionally, news has been published in print; when the transition first to digital, and then from digital to the internet, happened the coverage problems started. What is published in the printed edition may not be published on the internet. What is published on the internet may not be published in the printed edition. Even worse, what's published in a digital edition via fee-based services may not be all the content from the printed edition – and not all from the web version either (if there is one). Equally confusing is when a commercial news database carries all the printed articles from a newspaper except those written by freelance journalists, without informing its users. Here we have the main problem: news search tools can be very bad at documenting what sources they include and which parts of these sources are being indexed. Even when they do have good documentation, you can still find lots of flaws.

Searching

Advanced search features

In professional search services there are many advanced and complex search features that can be utilized in different search scenarios. These have been covered extensively in Chapter 3. Sometimes you can be surprised by finding quite advanced search features in the internal search engines used by some media websites. You should try to take full advantage of whatever is offered in this respect. Especially interesting are proximity search and implementations of wild cards and truncation. There may be some advanced search options in free news search engines, but many of them have no advanced search form or special syntax at all. The biggest of the news search engines tend to have a certain common set of search features, reflecting the fact that they index news on the web.

If an advanced search form does exist it will frequently have individual search boxes for applying basic search logic. One box may have an implicit AND operator, allowing you to enter all the words that you want to match. Another box will let you enter optional words, implying an OR operator. Some also have a search box where you can enter words that you don't want to find, implying the NOT operator. Normally there is also a separate search box for entering phrases. Preferably, you should also be able to search within the titles or headlines of news stories – this will probably be accomplished via a drop-down list of choices including at least 'in the title' and 'in the text'. If a means of searching for author names is offered you should be wary of the fact that they can sometimes be incorrect. This particular feature will work best if the search engine indexes RSS versions, because these have explicit author information taken from the source.

There may also be filters that will let you search for stories from an individual source or a website URL. These are extraordinarily useful because they enable you to examine the content of specific sources. If feed results or email alerts are supported you can use these to monitor sources for the appearance of keywords. Limiting by language is also a great feature, especially if you can choose several at once. Looking at results lists after choosing a particular language will give you ample opportunity to evaluate how well the news search engine's automatic language detection works. Filtering by country or region is trickier to implement and you can expect to find quite a lot of inconsistencies here. All types of filters will be of varying quality and you should probably concentrate on evaluating the type of filter that you find most useful for your own searches.

Post-search options to refine your results are valuable tools that allow you either to focus or to broaden your search. It's not uncommon that news search engines will let you refine by source, by topic or by the names of persons or organizations. You should try to evaluate the usefulness of these refining options, particularly for topics and names. The latter operation is commonly accomplished by using some form of named entity recognition as an aid to clustering. The outcome of these procedures can vary significantly. Sometimes search engines also offer related terms or synonyms, and these can occasionally provide great results.

Sorting options are very important and you should be able to alter the sorting order. In some rare cases there is a default sorting that can't be changed at all, which will be either by relevance or in chronological order with the newest first. This is a real handicap and you should complain to the search engine team about it. Most frequently, however, you can choose between relevance and chronological order. While this will be sufficient most of the time, sometimes you may want to sort the results chronologically with the oldest articles first. Some news search engines support this, but they are in a minority. Another good feature is the ability to turn off the clustering of search results and order them chronologically with possible duplicates visible.

Spelling correction and suggest functionality

A very popular feature in search engines is automatic spelling correction. This can be implemented in various ways such as by static links or a suggest functionality that is active while you type your search words. The latter is probably the most useful and can speed up the search process considerably. Suggestions will be generated from words that have been indexed and are common in the search engine's document collection. The lack of any functionality in this area is a very negative point in an evaluation. A good example of this functionality can be found in the PubMed search form Single Citation Matcher when searching Journal Title (Figure 5.1).

Personalization and customization

Many of the features that are today called personalization are in fact customization. We'll explain the distinction

| Figure 5.1 | When searching in the Single Citation Matcher of the medical database PubMed you get suggestions of journal titles. This is a very clever and handy functionality, as many journals have quite long and similar titles |

PubMed Single Citation Matcher

| PubMed | Nucleotide | Protein |

Click here! **New** Try the new Citation Matcher

Citation Search has been added to the PubMed **Advanced Search**

- Use this tool to find PubMed citations. You may omit any field.
- Journal may be the full title or the title abbreviation.
- For first and last author searching, use smith jc format.

Journal: jour

Date:

Volume:

Author n

Title wor

Go Cle

The Journal of biological chemistry
The New England journal of medicine
JAMA : the journal of the American Medical Association
Journal of immunology (Baltimore, Md. : 1950)
The American journal of physiology
The Biochemical journal
Journal of bacteriology
British medical journal
The Journal of urology
The Medical journal of Australia

between the two concepts. Personalization learns about you from your actions and behaviour. It's based on your implicit interests, while customization is based on your explicit interests. Personalization is very popular with search engines; Google, for example, uses your web history to promote websites in the results lists. This feature will be active by default unless you have turned off the saved web history in your browser.

Customization requires you to specify your interests or what you want, as when you edit your personal home page settings in services such as iGoogle, My Yahoo!, Netvibes or Pageflakes. Confusingly, in many cases the term 'personalization' is used for both explicit procedures as in customization and implicit processes as in personalization.

Important to evaluate here, of course, is what possibilities you have for doing your own customization and whether some personalization is done behind the scenes. If personalization is present, how easy is it to understand how it works? Can it easily be turned off? Does the personalization do things you don't want? Can it be an integrity problem for you as a user? What is the quality of the personalization? It's not that easy to evaluate personalization that's performed behind the scenes and that is based on criteria that aren't publicly available and that introduce a secret ingredient into the relevance algorithm.

One type of personalization that most search engines do today is automatic country recognition via client IP addresses. Let's say that you live in a country where English is not the native language, while you may be very fluent in English or in another language that you often use when on the internet. In such a case country recognition can be very irritating. Even if it is possible to change language and country in the preferences of the search engine, it will be specific to the computer on which you select your preferences because it's typically based on cookie files. Another solution apart from cookies is to do the customization after having created an account within the service. This is available in many but not all search services – there needs to be some means by which the search engine can receive your active choices and save them. When evaluating different search services you should look for what choices they offer.

Results

Clustering

An increasingly popular technology in recent years in news search is clustering. The same news event (not a broader topic or subject) is often referred to by many different newspapers. In order to group these articles together many free news search engines use some form of clustering. Clustering has existed for a long time in regular search engines so as to avoid polluting the results lists with multiple hits from the same site. If there are more than one hit from a site they are sorted together and can be reached via a link with a name such as 'More hits from the same website'. In news search this method is used to group articles relating to the same issue or event into the same cluster.

One article about the event will sometimes be more prominently featured, with a picture, while there are merely links to the other articles. There will also be a link to all of the articles within the cluster. Clustering is a great method to get better sorting of news search results. However, this technology doesn't always work properly. You can evaluate this easily by checking whether all the clustered articles are in fact about the same event. The way in which the clustering decides whether or not a story is about the same issue is sometimes debatable. One particular event can produce other news-related events – and where should the line be drawn when one issue has changed into another?

Duplicate detection

Duplicate control is a crucial feature when cross-searching several bibliographic databases. There are overlaps in coverage between many databases because they index the same source publications. With duplicate detection you'll avoid getting two or more copies of the same article in the results list. In the context of news search you have a duplicate problem when the same story with exactly the same content is present in several news sources. This typically happens when a news agency story is republished in multiple newspapers and on many media websites. Preferably, the original article – in this case from the news agency – should be the one visible in the search results list. This is seldom the case, however, and particularly so in free news search engines that use clustering to implement some degree of duplicate detection.

Regardless of what type of search service you use and how it implements duplicate control, it's important that you should be able to choose to see all duplicates if you want to. In some of the professional search services you can choose between several degrees of duplicate detection. This gives you even better possibilities for evaluating and finding the most efficient degree for the search that you're currently working with.

Subject categorization

Traditional manual subject categorization can be achieved in several different ways. There can be controlled vocabularies and there can be uncontrolled subject headings, as in tagging performed by users. Tagging is extremely popular on social websites. In most cases a subject categorization using a controlled vocabulary is more useful because it's generally hierarchical and it can also solve problems with synonyms, homonyms and polysemic words. However, controlled vocabularies are much more demanding of resources and difficult to maintain when every single subject – not just broader topics, such as medicine – has to have its own heading.

Controlled vocabularies also present problems in keeping up with recent developments. One example is the controlled MeSH vocabulary used for medical terms. The MeSH subject heading 'cellular phone' was introduced as recently as 2003 (Figure 5.2). Choosing subject headings is normally done by humans, frequently by indexing experts such as librarians. Using the tagging model, you can allow users to choose any words they like.

It is possible to implement some control over indexing or tagging by users by letting them choose from a prepared list of words, such as a controlled vocabulary. Preparing and updating a list of subject headings is one thing. There is the separate problem of choosing the most suitable subject

Figure 5.2   **The subject heading 'cellular phone' was introduced into the MeSH thesaurus as recently as 2003**

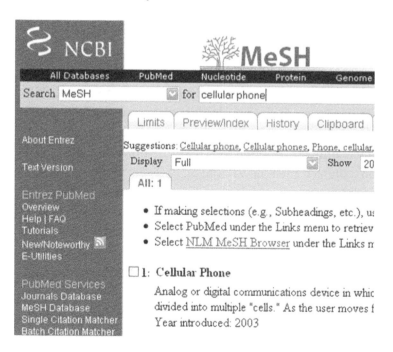

headings from that list when indexing. Having experts do the indexing of news stories, which are published in great quantities around the clock all over the world, is, of course, very time consuming. It's also very expensive when librarians and other experts do it and are paid for their efforts.

Allowing users to do the indexing by assigning tags of their own choosing is a form of crowd-sourcing and involves no cost all, but what about the quality? Some argue that if there are many people tagging the same articles you will be able to extract valuable information, even from tagging done by non-experts. Tagging advocates often correctly point out that it's not only non-experts who are tagging – many experts are doing it too. Some news and blog search engines try to extract tagging information in order to improve their subject categorization. This is most frequently done from blog posts, because it's much rarer to find tags assigned to news articles. However some news search engines do let users tag the articles shown in their results lists. These tags can then be used to enhance their categorizations.

Instead of having experts or normal users do indexing or tagging, search engines can also implement categorization automatically by having computer programs do it. Many free news search engines do this, and some do it better than others. Applying broader subject terms such as 'sports' and 'entertainment' is often very easy to do. For example, you can connect each news source or each section of a news source to a subject. If you know that the writing in La Gazetta dello sport is exclusively about sports you can choose to categorize all its articles under Sports. If it's easily established where on a news website the sports news is published you can match all content found there with the category Sports. For instance, Ekstra Bladet Sport has its sport articles under the URL http://ekstrabladet.dk/sport/.

There are many more or less advanced algorithms that are used in news search engines and of course many of them are similar to normal web search engine algorithms. Some analyse inbound links, link anchor texts and texts that are found close to them. They can also use probabilistic algorithms and other related mechanisms. In order to evaluate the subject categorization of a news search tool you need to browse the subjects and see whether they do indeed show news articles relevant to the subject. You'll probably have to do it quite extensively in order to tell how well it's working. If the quantity of irrelevant news stories becomes very high you can conclude that browsing the news in this way is not very helpful in that search engine. On the other hand, subject categorization can often be a useful complement to free text search.

If you search for your favourite soccer team using its full name, such as West Bromwich Albion, for example, you may not find all the articles that use nicknames or acronyms such as West Brom or WBA. Sometimes query-expanding algorithms in the news search engine will solve this. Of course, there can also be cases where a relevant article never actually mentions the name of the team but instead discusses soccer teams in the Black Country. A subject categorization that works really well will capture those articles too.

Translations

Some news search tools offer the opportunity to get a machine translation of a page by clicking a link. Of course, it won't be a perfect translation, but if you already have some understanding from taking a second or third language in school you can probably work it out. Some people do say that a rough translation is better than none at all. If the news search engine lack links for quick translation another possibility is to manually use Google Translate, for instance while using Yahoo! News. To do this you will have to copy and paste the article text or supply the URL of the page.

RSS feeds and email alerts

In our opinion this is something that can make a world of difference. The possibility to automate searches and monitor them through an RSS reader is of vital importance to many users. Other users prefer to use alerts and this is also something that we value highly. When evaluating news search engines you'll probably consider the ability to receive search results in these ways to be a major advantage. If you have very distinctive keywords this function can actually be more important than a full set of advanced search features.

6

Keeping track of the blogosphere

Abstract: An early form of blog emerged in the mid 1990s, but blogging really began to take off when easy-to-use blogging software started to appear at the end of the decade and the current familiar blog format with comments, links and tags began to develop. Specialized tools have been developed for searching blogs, among them Google Blog Search, Bloglines, Technorati, BlogPulse and Twingly. They offer advanced search features and some interesting display features, such as trend graphs and statistical information. Blog directories are categorized lists of blogs that can be browsed or searched by keywords to find interesting blogs.

Key words: blog search, blog directories, blogging, blogosphere.

Introduction

Blogging has become a very popular form of publishing on the internet and some of the most interesting stories are told by bloggers. The discussion about the credibility of the blogger, initiated by journalists, is still ongoing but is maybe not so aggressive as it used to be. Many professionals within the media world have embraced the blog format and newspapers and other news sites have started featuring their own blogs. In this chapter we try to find a working definition of what a blog is, trace the history and explosion of blogging, and outline the still expanding blogosphere. A short history of blog searching leads to a description of the most important blog search engines and blog directories that are currently available. These include, among others, Google Blog Search, Bloglines, Technorati, BlogPulse, IceRocket and Twingly.

What exactly is a blog?

It's not all that easy to define exactly what a blog is. However, there are many common elements in the various definitions that are floating around. To start with the name, a blog was originally called a weblog. That is, weblog as in web-log, which in itself tells us a little something about what it is. Like the log book of a captain at sea, it can be an account of an actual journey. Mostly, though, it's a kind of account of the mental journey of the person who writes it. Many blogs consist of comments about things the authors have read about on the web. This is the etymology behind the word weblog, describing a journey on the web.

The author of a blog is called a blogger, which similarly is short for weblogger – but that form of the word isn't used very much any more. The act of writing a blog is called blogging. When a blogger writes about a certain topic he or she blogs about it. The corpus of web publishing where writers use a blog format is frequently referred to as the blogosphere. All kinds of interesting and not so interesting phenomena related to blogging have acquired names that are made up from some form of the word blog, and which you will soon learn.

Before we delve further into such matters we should first stop to describe the characteristics of the blog format. In fact the very anatomy of blogs is perhaps what defines blogging and what differentiates it from other types of web publishing. Most blogs are updated very frequently, as much as several times per day, but mostly it's daily or maybe a couple of times every week. The home page of the blog invariably has a number of chronologically arranged articles or blog posts, as they're commonly called.

What makes the blog different from a normal log is that the blog posts are always presented in reverse chronological order. This means that the most current post is always the first, at the top of the home page. Then other blog posts follow, becoming progressively older as you scroll down the page. All blog posts carry a date, and typically the hour of day when they were published. This makes it easy to tell how current the writing is. To aid the navigation of the blog there are usually archive links to all the posts that you don't see on the home page of the blog.

There are lots of other features that are prevalent in blogs today, but the ones already mentioned are really all that are needed to have a working definition of the blog format. The first weblogs where created manually using HTML – and you can do it this way even now. However, the main reason why blogging has become so ubiquitous and such an immensely popular form of web publishing is that you don't have to know any HTML to start blogging.

It was with the appearance of really good weblogging software that the process of writing a blog became so easy. In fact it made it possible for almost anyone with an internet connection to do it. People without knowledge of HTML or indeed any desire to acquire such knowledge can now start a weblog within minutes and get on with their writing without too much effort. Without the right software to facilitate this, blogging would never have caught on in a big way and become such a huge success all over the world. Therefore the very simplicity of blogging is another important characteristic to add to our definition.

The roots of blogging

So how did it all start and how did the blogging craze come about? Some blog historians claim that the page with links to new websites that was maintained by the actual creator of the World Wide Web, Tim Berners-Lee, was in fact a forerunner to the weblog. The What's New page of Marc Andreesen, creator of the first graphical web browser, Mosaic, is considered to be another. Very early on, during the formative years of the web, many web diaries, online journals, e-zines and other related forms also saw the light of day.

Some of the earliest web pages that start to fit our description include Justin Hall's Links from the Underground (1994), Michael Sippey's Filtered for Purity (1997) and Steve Bogart's News, Pointers and Commentary (1998). Common to all these was that they featured links to other web pages that had caught the attention of the writers and which they thought would be of interest to their readers.

Back then, these were called filter blogs because of the way in which the writers became a kind of filter, presenting their most interesting discoveries on the web. They wrote logs of their travels on the web, creating convenient filters for their readers. So here is yet another typical feature of the blog in action – extensive linking to other places on the web. This made weblogs different from most other web pages at the time, where the writers wanted their audience to stay browsing the same website.

A seminal figure in blog history is the pioneering computer programmer Dave Winer, who founded the UserLand company. His blog is called Scripting News and was started in 1996. He also wrote the Manila publishing software and conceived the blog publishing platform called Radio UserLand. Winer has continued to play a crucial part in the later evolution of blogs and blog-related forms. He was not, however, the person who came up with the word 'weblog'.

That person is considered to be John Barger, who maintained a website called Robot Wisdom. It was there that he coined the term 'weblog' for websites like his own that provided links with commentaries and news filtering. In 1998 he estimated that there were some 30 websites doing this kind of thing and he also wrote that they seemed to form a social network, linking to each other. Some say that this was the germ that spawned the worldwide blogosphere of the millions upon millions of blogs that we have today.

Another early blog, started in 1998, was written by Cameron Barrett and called CamWorld. From 1999 he provided a list of other similar sites that he visited often. This list appeared on the left of the screen, alongside the blog posts. This practice soon became another staple of the blog world and is called a blogroll. In their blogrolls bloggers typically point to other blogs similar to their own. These are the blogs that are read by and frequently linked to by the blogger and which the writer thinks will be interesting for his or her readers as well. Peter Merholz was one of the readers of CamWorld and decided that he would henceforth call weblogs 'wee-blogs'. This word was soon discarded for the shorter and catchier word 'blog'.

The blog explosion

The next and the most important phase in the evolution of blogging was the blog publishing platforms with easy-to-use blogging software that started to appear from 1999 onwards. First came Andrew Smale's Pitas.com, which had only two boxes that the blogger had to fill in to write blog posts, one box for the link and one box for the commentary.

Really simple. But **Blogger.com**, which was later acquired by Google, made it even simpler and this is where the explosion started. Blogger was the brain-child of blog luminaries Evan Williams and Meg Hourihan of the San Francisco-based PyraLabs company. They initially offered a single box where you did all your writing. If you wanted a link, you had to write it yourself. In a way this probably steered blogging away from the original concept of links with commentaries and opened up other possible uses of the blog format.

Another extremely popular blog publishing platform that was launched in 1999 is **LiveJournal**, which is still one of the biggest. But it was back at Blogger.com that the next invention, which is at the core of the blogging world today, was presented. In 2000 it introduced the so-called permalink, which is a permanent link to individual blog posts. Before this it was very difficult to link in a practical way to individual posts, thus making them kind of anonymous. With the permalink this obstacle was overcome and with it came extended possibilities for citing bloggers and commenting on what they wrote, while linking explicitly to their stories. The connections between blogs and bloggers increased enormously because of this simple glue.

During this time the blog platforms started to enable the readers of blogs to write their own comments on individual blog posts. Blog comments are yet another of the characteristic traits of the blog format that we know today. To comment on something that a blogger had written you now simply had to click on the comment link and start firing away.

In some cases the blog comments would be published immediately on the blog site itself. The most common procedure, however, was for the comments to be moderated by the blogger. This was initially considered to be a cowardly practice on the part of the blogger, but it soon became more of a necessity. The reason for this is the ever-present blog-comment spamming that unfortunately is so frequent these days. The fact that many bloggers are very popular and their websites often get high rankings in search engine results lists makes them perfect targets for spamming.

A new way to connect bloggers even more appeared a few years later, with the introduction of the trackback comment. This was introduced by another San Francisco-based outfit, called Six Apart, which also created **Movable Type**, one of the most popular blog software programs. With trackbacks a blogger can automatically alert another blogger when he or she comments on and links to a blog post on the other blogger's site. In this way readers could easily find comments on blog posts both on the blog's website and on other blog websites as well. It's estimated that around 50 per cent of all bloggers use some form of trackback implementation.

Around this time open source-based blog programs started to appear and the first of these was called Greymatter. Later on came the popular **WordPress** program and anyone was now able to download high-quality blog software with which to experiment for free. However, most writers used web-based solutions where you didn't have to install any software and could concentrate on getting on with the writing. There are plenty of such blogging services where you can start blogging almost instantly, such as Blogger, LiveJournal, Wordpress.com, **Typepad** and through **Windows Live Spaces**. In 2009 **Technorati** reported that more than half of all bloggers used a free third-party blog-hosting service.

The blogosphere

Trying to find out how big today's blogosphere is presents many difficulties. All kinds of figures circulate in the media and various scientific and non-scientific investigations have been conducted during the last few years. A good place to start looking for some indication of the size of the blogosphere and who the bloggers are is in the annual reports called *State of the Blogosphere* published by the blog search engine Technorati.

Since 2004 David Sifry of Technorati has compiled various topical statistics concerning different aspects of the blogging world and these are probably the most comprehensive source for such information. The methods used by Technorati to assemble its data sets have been criticized by some people, but the fact remains that they are currently the best that can be found. In 2008 Technorati stated that it had indexed 133 million blogs since 2002 and 1.5 million of the blogs that it indexed had published at least one blog post during the last seven days.

In October 2009 Sifry published the latest results in the series of *State of the Blogosphere* reports on Technorati.com. Here are some of the findings from these reports, which were compiled using both surveys and search engine statistics:

- 67 per cent of all bloggers are men
- 60 per cent are between 18 and 40 years old
- bloggers generally have received higher education
- more than 50 per cent are married and have children.

Interestingly 35 per cent of the survey respondents had a background in or currently worked within the traditional media. Twenty per cent updated their blogs from mobile devices and the typical posting frequency was two or three times per week.

The most common tags used to categorize blog posts were words such as politics, blogging, technology, friends, business, family, entertainment, movies and books. Many of the bloggers regularly post media content on their blog, including photos (82 per cent), video (more than 50 per cent) and music or spoken audio (a little more than 10 per cent). More than 80 per cent use comments, have built-in syndication through RSS or Atom and have archives by date and/or tags. Of the bloggers who answered that they had built-in syndication, 75 per cent also made their full content available in this way.

A lot has been written about blogs and their relation to traditional journalism. Can blogs be viewed as a new kind of news source? What is their credibility? Some journalists embrace the blog form while others think very little of it. There are many journalists who consider bloggers to be charlatans not worthy of all the attention they get. In the society of blogs, as in the traditional media, there are few leaders and many followers. The A-list of blogs includes the websites of some extremely popular and influential bloggers. These are the ones that are read by, commented on and linked to by the many.

The influence of blogs is undeniable, whatever you might think about the bloggers. Blogging has become extremely widespread and has made a great impact even in countries where outspoken bloggers are being actively persecuted. The free blogging platforms have enabled people in countries such as China and Iran to publish stories that the government can't control. This has led to a new war on the freedom of speech that involves building sophisticated firewalls and filters, which are being installed at critical network nodes and internet cafes. The international non-governmental organization **Reporters Sans Frontières** is tirelessly investigating and writing about matters such as these and regularly reports about cases where bloggers have been persecuted and even imprisoned. Its website and the network of bloggers from around the globe called **Global Voices Online** are the best places to find information about bloggers living under repression and to read stories that don't appear in mainstream media. Insightful comments concerning blogging and internet censorship can also be found in former CNN Beijing correspondent Rebecca McKinnon's blog, **RConversation.**

Another worrying aspect of the blogosphere is the proliferation of spam blogs or 'splogs' as they are also called. These are fake or inauthentic blogs that are automatically generated by procedures such as 'scraping' original content from authentic blogs and republishing it in subtly altered forms. The goal is to create blogs that seem real and have interesting texts but are actually only vehicles to increase the page ranking of other sites in Google results lists. This is not the same thing as blog comment spamming, where you take advantage of the page ranking of a real blog by writing innocent-looking comments with links to the sites that you want to promote. However, the purpose is the same and search engines are having a hard time trying to deal with these problems. Already in 2005 a random test conducted by Blogoscoped.com of 50 blogs hosted by Google at the Blogspot.com domain showed that 60 per cent of the blogs tested were spam blogs. After a further 100 Blogspot.com blogs were tested the figure decreased to 42 per cent, but that doesn't alter the fact that this is a huge problem.

The evolution of blog searching

The need for specialized tools for searching and finding interesting blogs became apparent during the first few years of the new millennium. The earliest attempt at providing a good way to find blogs was probably the blog directory created by blog pioneer Brigitte Eaton. It was originally called the Eatonweb Portal and after 10 years it is still very much alive and is now called the **Eatonweb Blog Directory**. In its infancy it listed some 50 blogs, but the directory rapidly expanded to include thousands of blogs sorted by categories such as subjects, languages and countries. Lately, Eatonweb staff have concentrated their efforts on developing metrics and indicators to rate the importance of the blogs included in the directory. In doing this they are putting an emphasis on quality. A long-standing directory of news sources, called **NewsIsFree**, was launched in 2000 and has from the very beginning listed quality blogs as alternative news sources.

Several of the first projects that acknowledged the importance of blogs were about trying to find out how information spread on the internet. Cameron Marlowe of MIT Media Laboratory created **Blogdex**, which was an attempt to list news articles that were most frequently linked to by bloggers. Marlowe called this project, which he did for his thesis, a weblog diffusion index, in which he created top lists of news stories and links to blog posts that cited them (Figure 6.1). For this purpose he used a search engine spider

---

Figure 6.1   Blogdex – the weblog diffusion index

THE WEBLOG DIFFUSION INDEX - HTTP://BLOGDEX.NET

The following sites are the most contagious information currently spreading in the weblog community.

1. MSNBC - U.S. Army report on Iraqi prisoner abuse
    msnbc.msn.com/id/4894001
    » track this site | 33 links

2. The Shining in 30 seconds with bunnies.
    angryalien.com/0504/shiningbunnies.html
    » track this site | 18 links

3. Disney Forbidding Distribution of Film That Criticizes Bush
    nytimes.com/2004/05/05/national/05DISN.html
    » track this site | 17 links

that initially visited 9,000 blogs. The website was discontinued in 2006 but some of these top lists can still be studied in the Internet Archive using a search for the address blogdex.net.

A related project was Shanti Bradford's **Popdex**, which in a similar fashion created top lists of websites that were linked to by the blogs indexed by his search engine spider. He called Popdex a website popularity index and it was an excellent place to find out what was hot on the internet on a day-by-day basis. Unfortunately, a lot of spam articles appeared on Popdex, making it less useful, and it is now an abandoned project.

The first real blog search engine, **Daypop**, appeared in 2001 and was the brain-child of American programmer Dan Chan (Figure 6.2). Having lived in Hong Kong and encountered difficulties trying to follow the chaotic US presidential elections, he decided to create his own search engine. His purpose was to make it easier to find news stories and blog commentaries on them. Daypop was a hybrid between a news search engine and a blog search engine and it was possible to restrict your search to either type of source if you wanted to.

Chan also included various top lists, such as the most popular news articles among bloggers, the most popular

Figure 6.2   Daypop was the first major blog search engine

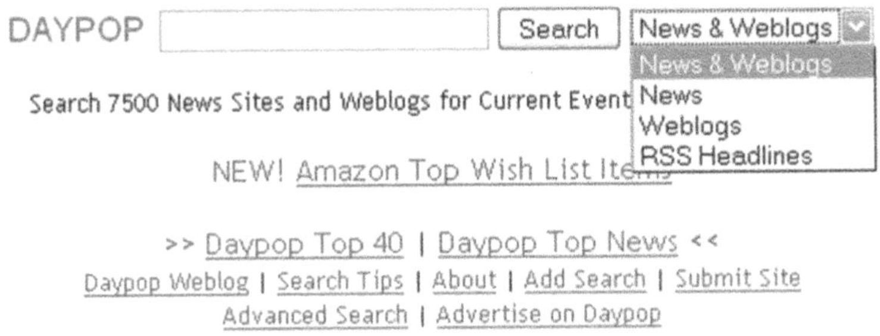

DAYPOP [ ] [Search] [News & Weblogs ▼]

Search 7500 News Sites and Weblogs for Current Event

News & Weblogs
News
Weblogs
RSS Headlines

NEW! Amazon Top Wish List Items

>> Daypop Top 40 | Daypop Top News <<
Daypop Weblog | Search Tips | About | Add Search | Submit Site
Advanced Search | Advertise on Daypop

blog posts and the most popular links. Another one was top word bursts, which was a list of words the use of which had suddenly increased in the articles that Daypop indexed. The search engine also provided links to blogs similar or related to the ones listed in the results lists, thus making it easier to find more interesting reading.

It was the combination of two dedicated blog search engines that created the model for the blog search engines to come. Two similar projects that started in Massachusetts resulted in the twin search engines Feedster and rssSearch that were ultimately combined in 2003, adopting the **Feedster** name. This was a very powerful search engine for blog searching only and had lots of interesting features. For instance, it sported cached copies like Daypop, offered search alerts via email and even had a web-based RSS reader called MyFeedster where you could subscribe to blogs. It also supported OPML files, so you could save your blog subscriptions and export them to another news aggregator. Finally, it had very advanced search syntax that the blog searcher could use. Sadly, Scott Johnson's Feedster was terminated in 2007.

The most important blog search engines

Google Blog Search – plain vanilla blog searching

After these historical remarks it's time to take a look at the best blog search engines currently available. It should be noted that most blogs have an embedded search box that offers simple keyword searching within the blog posts. If you use this you won't benefit from the additional search features that come with the indexing performed by the blog search engines. Many people will probably prefer to use Google Blog Search because of the dominant role that Google plays in everyday web searching. Maybe you think 'why look any further?' if you already use Google for web searching. The chances are that you will reconsider, because there are many features that you won't find in Google Blog Search that are available in other blog search engines.

Curiously, it took Google a surprisingly long time to actually launch a blog search engine at all. This seemed strange to many people, considering that Google bought the most popular blogging platform, Blogger.com, as early as 2003. Many assumed that Google would quickly come out with its own blog search engine because of this. Google Blog Search first appeared as a beta test version two and a half years later. As for many of Google's specialized search engines, it took another couple of years before it finally emerged from the beta stage in 2009.

Google Blog Search has a home page which is very like its older sister, Google News. Using advanced clustering, Google Blog Search automatically generates headlines and lead paragraphs for 10 stories that it presents with images to illustrate them. The bigger stories have clusters of blog posts with similar content, in the same way as Google News. There can be literally hundreds of blog posts in the first few clusters. To the left you find 12 categories, such as Politics, World, US, Technology, Entertainment and Science. To the right you have 'Hot queries', which provides links to the current most frequently used search expressions. In the section 'Recent posts', under the queries, you will find the latest blog posts that have been indexed.

The Advanced Search form in Google Blog Search has a section with a blue background in which you will find tools to search for individual blog posts. There are five search boxes that you can use to create standard search expressions without resorting to special syntax. Search words that you want to find in a blog post can be entered in the first search box, called 'with all of these words'. This indicates an implicit AND operator between the search words. The next search box is for phrase searching, which could otherwise be accomplished using quotation marks around your search phrase.

If you have several search words and are happy for any one of them appear in the results you can use the third search box. This is the equivalent of using an OR operator between search words. The fourth search box is for words that you want to exclude from your search, which is the same as using a NOT operator. Finally, you have the option to search only in the titles of the blog posts, which is an excellent way to focus your search. By doing this you will retrieve significantly fewer search results, which can often be desirable.

The section below the one with the blue background enables you to use a few other search parameters. If you want to search for words in blog titles rather than in the titles of individual posts there is a search box here for that. It will yield very unpredictable results, considering all the strange names that people tend to give their blogs. The next search box is for entering the address or URL of a specific blog. This way you can restrict your search to a specific blog.

The search for specific authors is more interesting because, contrary to web pages, blog posts have explicit author information that can be indexed. You can also use the tools for specifying date ranges with confidence. Doing the same thing in a general web search engine will produce many incorrect results because there is no reliable date information in normal web pages. Results lists can be sorted either by date or by relevance, which is the default. Just as in Google News, you can subscribe to the searches using RSS feeds or email alerts.

Bloglines – reliable and extended search facilities

It is somewhat surprising that neither Microsoft nor Yahoo! provides its own dedicated blog search engine. Only for a short period during 2005 to 2006 did Yahoo! News include results from blogs and the option to search for blog results separately. We have to look to the fourth-largest US search engine, Ask.com, for our next blog search engine. Ask.com was originally a natural language search and answers database called AskJeeves. Today it has an advanced general search engine using web search technology developed by the Teoma project at Rutgers University. For its blog search, however, it uses technology acquired in connection with the purchase of Bloglines in 2005. This popular blog search engine and web-based RSS feed aggregator was originally launched in 2003.

In 2006 Ask.com presented its own version of blog search, combining its in-house relevance ranking with data from the Bloglines search engine. Originally prominently featured as Ask Blog & Feed Search, by 2010 it seems to have been discontinued. So now we turn instead to **Bloglines.com,** where the original blog search engine still operates separately. At Bloglines searching is not emphasized as much as the feed aggregator aspect. You'll find a simple search box at the top right of the page. There you can only choose to search for articles or for feeds, but there is a link to more options for searching. Using this you can enter the normal Bloglines aggregator interface with the Search tab active.

It's here that you will find the Advanced Search form with all the interesting options that the search engine supports (Figure 6.3). Starting with feed search, you get several search boxes that can be combined and where you can enter search words using basic search logic. Here you get drop-down

Figure 6.3 The Advanced Search form in Bloglines

choices to search for all of the words or any of the words, to exclude words or to search for a phrase, as in Google Blog Search. You can also make decisions as to where you want to find or not find words or phrases.

The default is to search anywhere in the blog posts. Using the drop-down list you can also restrict your search to titles of feeds and, more interestingly, to the descriptions of the feeds (all blogs have a description where the writer can enter a few sentences explaining what the blog is all about). This gives a lot more precision than merely searching for feed titles. Additionally, you can search for the email address of the editor of the blog, which can be useful too. You can also search for posts at a specific blog using the URL. Below the search boxes you can restrict your search to one or more languages. Currently there are some 20 languages to choose from, and you can create your own set of languages to be searched simultaneously.

When searching for individual posts you have the same search boxes for basic search logic, but now you have a few other choices concerning where to find your search terms. 'In the title' means in the titles of the individual blog posts rather than in feed titles, and again, this can be a good way to focus your search. Then there is the author search, which is more powerful than the editor email search used for feed searching. Remember that a blog can have several different writers. Additionally, there are menu choices enabling you to search for words in subjects and in citations, but exactly how these work is not apparent.

In the area below the search boxes we again find the option to restrict the search to a set of languages of your own choice. Then comes the Limits section, which is where you can use the integration with Bloglines aggregator data. You have the option to search with no limits, search your own feeds (if you use Bloglines as an aggregator), search everything except your own feeds and even search the public feeds that some other Bloglines user subscribes to. To sum it all up, you have the ability to discover things in your own feeds or in the feeds of other users, such as maybe your friends, or to use Bloglines as a normal search engine with the possibility of excluding your own feeds. You can also decide on date restrictions and choose to include or exclude news feeds, as opposed to blog feeds.

You can sort the results lists by relevance, by popularity and also by date filtered by feed popularity. The last option will enable you to exclude posts from feeds that have fewer than two subscribers among Bloglines users, or you can require that the feeds have many subscribers. Under the hits themselves you have links to various functions of general use. 'More info' shows you how many subscribers the feed of the post has in Bloglines and how many in-links or citations the post itself has. 'Email post' of course lets you email the post to a friend.

'Clip post' is really good because with this you can save the address of the post in a little note that is kept on the Bloglines server. 'Preview feed' opens the feed in a preview window, allowing you to have a glimpse at the content without actually visiting the originating blog. The last link will enable you to subscribe to the feed within your aggregator account at Bloglines. All in all, the Bloglines search engine offers many practical functions, advanced search options, seamless integration with the aggregator and a mature interface. It is therefore highly recommended.

Technorati – at the forefront of the movement

Earlier in this chapter we mentioned Technorati as a source of statistical information on the blogosphere. At the Technorati website there's also a blog search engine and it's the data from this that is used for the various reports on blogging that are published there. Here you'll also find interesting feature articles on blogging, in-depth interviews with bloggers and the Technorati blog itself. All of these offer valuable insights concerning the evolution of the blogging world, and the people who write blogs and their motivations. If you're at all interested in these matters here is an excellent selection of reading. Technorati also hosts the online community of blog writers called Blogcritics.org, which produces high-quality, award-winning reviews, commentaries and news stories. Blogcritics is indexed as a news source by, among others, Google News and its articles are syndicated through Newstex.

Technorati was launched in late 2002 and was originally created by David Sifry for the purpose of writing an article on blogging in collaboration with the editor of the Linux Journal. The blog search engine for the project soon added many new features, and in 2004 claimed to have indexed 286 million blog posts. The search engine index grew rapidly over the years and started to include all kinds of top lists in the same manner as Daypop, Blogdex and Popdex. It soon became the largest search engine for searching blogs and a great data source for information on various aspects of the blogging movement. Technorati continues to play a very active role in the blogging world. It also claims to have the largest social media advertising network and presents itself as a full service media company.

If we look at the search engine itself, it has fewer advanced search features than Bloglines but has the bigger index of the two. From the home page you can make a simple search either for feeds or for articles. Having done an initial search you get the option to refine your search. This opens up an advanced search form where you can add a couple of restrictions to your search. These include selecting a topic from a list of nine broad categories such as entertainment, politics, business, sports and science. You can also choose to search only blogs, only news feeds or a combination of the two. Technorati is a hybrid between a blog search engine and news search engine, in the same way as Daypop was. An interesting way to filter your search results in Technorati is by choosing high, medium or low Authority (Figure 6.4).

Authority in Technorati is a measure of the influence and position of a blog within the blogosphere. The most

| Figure 6.4 | Filtering results by Authority while refining a search in Technorati |

150

important factor in the calculation of the Authority is linking patterns, and the number of ingoing links or citations is crucial, just as in Google PageRank. This metric is updated on a very frequent basis, so the value can vary considerably during relatively short time periods. Technorati Authority is supplemented by a ranking system in which blogs are ordered by their current Authority. There is also a general Top 100 list where you can look for quality blogs of all kinds. If you click to see the top lists for the different categories and their sub-categories you enter the Technorati Blog Directory, which we will return to in the section on blog directories.

Another distinguishing feature of Technorati is the way in which tags are used. Tags are words or phrases that are used by the writers of blogs to categorize their content. Not all bloggers care for tags, but most do. In fact Technorati reported in 2009 that 85 per cent of all the blogs it indexed used tags. Tags are a practical way to enhance browsing for the visitors to a blog. They are a key feature in what is called Web 2.0 and are used extensively on sites like delicious and Flickr. Technorati has a page with the most popular tags that have been used in blog posts over the last month. In this list you can click on tags and see the most recent posts to have these tags assigned to them. Tags are also used by the article writers on the Technorati website itself. In October 2009 Technorati was revamped and upgraded, with some functions not initially implemented – but they should all be available by the time you read this.

BlogPulse – the conversation tracker from Nielsen

If you are interested in the tracking and analysing of blog content one of the most interesting blog search engines is

BlogPulse. It was originally launched by the Intelliseek company, which was acquired by BuzzMetrics and later became a part of Nielsen, which is well known for its NetRatings market research analyses. There is a very pronounced emphasis on metrics and trend monitoring within the blogosphere in BlogPulse. The search engine tracks over 125 million blogs as of 2010. One of the attractions of BlogPulse is its array of top lists in which you can track conversation trends that have emerged within the most recent time frame.

There are five different forms for searching within the blogosphere at the top of the BlogPulse home page. Another way to search is by using its dedicated search page. If you want to keep it simple you can perform a basic search for keywords or URLs. Then there are the Advanced Search features that enable you to perform a search for all of the words that you enter, any of the words or an exact phrase. Additionally, there's a larger search box where you can employ standard Boolean search logic. Here you'll be able to construct complex queries using the operators AND, OR and NOT with phrases and single keywords. It's possible to use parentheses to group expressions and you can even use more than one layer of parentheses. This is a very powerful way to search if you're comfortable with using such syntax. You can also add exact date restrictions and decide whether the results should be ordered by date or by relevance.

One of the best tools in blog searching is the ability to search for posts linking to a certain web address. This can be accomplished by using the Link Search feature, which is good for finding posts that reference the home pages of websites or specific pages within them. A more specialized feature of the BlogPulse search engine is Trend Search. With this you can track trends using words, phrases or URLs. You can enter up to three different searches at the same time to look at a composite trend graph for them. The different queries will be outlined in the graph using different colours (Figure 6.5). The trend graphs generated in this way are clearly outlined, quickly displayed and can be saved to normal image files. The graphs are also clickable and you can click through to specific posting dates along the time axis. This is a very efficient way of finding specific events that have started conversations in the blogosphere.

The top lists displayed by BlogPulse on the home page can give a quick overview of what's hot on the internet at the moment. On the home page you get the top five of all these lists, but you can click to see the top 40. The eight featured lists on BlogPulse are Top Links, Top Blog Posts, Top News Stories, Top Blogs, Top News Sources, Top Videos, Key People and Key Phrases. All lists are generated from an automated analysis of the blog posts indexed by the search engine and are intended to reflect what bloggers think is most interesting, on a daily basis.

Figure 6.5 Trend Search graph generated by BlogPulse for three different soccer players

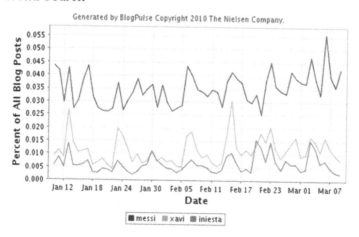

Twingly – blog search made in Sweden

Twingly from Sweden started in 2007, offering to newspapers to publish links to blogs about their articles. The first clients were the two biggest Swedish dailies, *Dagens Nyheter* and *Svenska Dagbladet*. This concept, which was called Twingly Blogstream, proved highly successful and Twingly now provides blog links to over 100 (mostly European) media websites in 11 languages. In June 2008 Twingly released its blog search engine to the general public. Twingly is noted for its ongoing efforts to develop an algorithm for a blog search free from spam blogs. The feature is currently in beta testing and you can try it out at the Twingly website.

The Twingly blog search engine has an Advanced Search form, which is the best place to start exploring. Here you can do all the normal stuff, such as searching for all of these words, any of these words, without these words or for an exact phrase. You can also search for blog posts from a specific blog either by name or using the blog's web address. Additionally, you can perform searches for blog posts that link to a certain web address such as a news article or another blog post. Restrictions by date ranges and language are possible.

Twingly's excellent online documentation of its search language enables you to learn about its special syntax for use in the basic search form. For instance, you can search for posts in several languages at once using an expression such as 'lang:en|de', which will return posts in English and German. One particularly interesting search mode (and a rarity among blog search engines) allows you to search using the tags that bloggers have assigned to their posts. For example, to search for posts that have been tagged with the word jazz use 'tag:jazz', and to search for several tags at once use 'tag:jazz|funk|soul'. Other special syntax that can be applied in this way are the prefixes blog:, site:, link:, tspan: (time-span) and approved: (for spam-free or non-spam-free filtering) (Figure 6.6).

The Advanced Search form has several sorting options. One of these is TwinglyRank, which is a blog ranking specific to each language. You can also sort by number of in-links to a post or a blog and by recommendations to a post or a blog. These can point to specific posts or to the web addresses of the blogs. The latter is the more interesting because you can see which blogs among the results are the most popular targets for linking. In the result views you have three sorting options: TwinglyRank (the default), date or in-links. From the results you can click through to blog Profiles, where you can write a recommendation for blogs that you find interesting. This provides data for the Recommendation sorting option and is Twingly's way of implementing a Web 2.0 flavour in the search.

Particularly interesting are Twingly's lists of top blogs in different languages, sorted by their TwinglyRank. In other blog search engines the top listings are completely dominated by English-language content, which means that you're never pointed to the most popular blogs in other languages. There are Top 100 lists for blogs in 12 languages, including Dutch, Greek, Portuguese and the Scandinavian languages Swedish, Finnish, Danish and Norwegian.

Figure 6.6 **Trying out the spam-free blogs filter in Twingly**

Blogscope – full-featured blog searching from Canada

The blog search engine and visualization tool Blogscope is the result of an ongoing research project at the University of Toronto. Several PhD students are contributing to the project, which is headed by Professor Nick Koudas. Currently Blogscope tracks over 40 million blogs and has indexed in the region of 1.2 billion blog posts. The aim of the project is to develop technology for extracting what public opinion has to say on a range of topics. The visualization component captures bursts of interest in the blogosphere along a dateline in a way that resembles BlogPulse. Widgets are available for embedding Blogscope visualized comparisons and trend graphs on your own website. The publicly accessible implementation of Blogscope, which you can use for free, is just a limited preview of the project's search engine technology.

The public version of Blogscope has lots of advanced search options. Searching is normally done from the search box in the upper right corner of the screen. Using this you're limited to entering keywords and choosing how results should be ranked. However, by clicking 'Options' and then 'Advanced options' you get a pop-up window where you can construct more complex queries. Below the simple search box there's a link to a Boolean search constructor page where you can type words or phrases that you want to include in or exclude from the search. You can also search by blog-hosting services, such as Blogspot, Livejournal, Live Spaces and Wordpress – you can type in any domain name you want.

The standard ranking or scoring gives some preference to more recent posts. You can boost the impact of recency on ranking or make it the sole ranking criterion. Two other ranking options are by relevance according either to the search engine or to the influence of the blogs. You can also combine recency and influence (Figure 6.7). This composite scoring principle is called 'Enhanced' in the Advanced Search form. You may want to experiment a bit with these settings to find what best suits your type of query. The next thing to consider is which index to use. There is blog standard, blog stemmed and news standard. If you use the index called blog stemmed, your search word will be converted to the root form and then expanded to all derivations of the word; it works only with English words.

Some other advanced search options are related to the time-span that you're interested in. You can set a start date and an end date for your search, or specify maximum and minimum ages for the posts you want to see. Blogscope's geographical awareness is evident in the next few options, which allow you to choose countries, provinces and even cities. The countries search box will guess as you start typing, so you don't have to type many characters before your country is suggested. The most exotic search parameter in the advanced options is by gender. Naturally, only two choices are offered – but we think these should be sufficient. How well it works is another question.

Figure 6.7 **Trying out different scoring options in Blogscope**

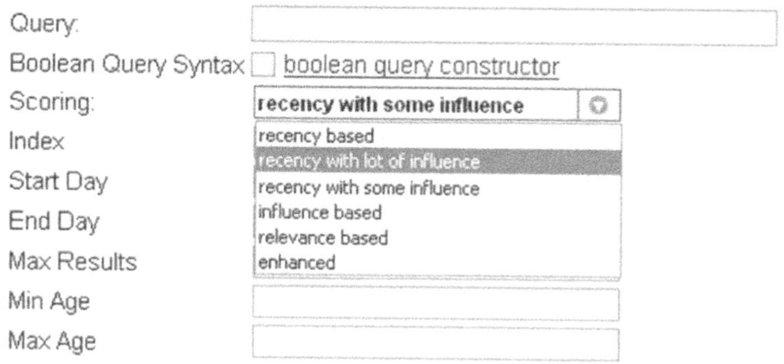

Query:	
Boolean Query Syntax	☐ boolean query constructor
Scoring:	recency with some influence
Index	recency based
	recency with lot of influence
Start Day	recency with some influence
End Day	influence based
	relevance based
Max Results	enhanced
Min Age	
Max Age	

You will find several interesting things in the results lists. For example, an icon indicates whether a post includes images, audio or video. To the right is a list of Related Terms. Three different types of search can be performed by clicking on a related term. The default is to add the related term to your search and use it as a filter within the results list. You can also use the related term instead of your own and search all documents in the index. The third option is to compare the popularity of your original search term and the related term.

Underneath the related terms is the popularity curve, which is a trend graph for your search query spanning the two last months. When you click on it you get a more detailed view and you can also choose other time spans. You do this either interactively or by choosing links for the last 3 or 6 months. Blogscope will also generate images of the popularity curve in sizes up to 600 × 400 pixels that you can embed in your own website. The necessary HTML code is provided in a window to the left. To work interactively with the graphs, position the cursor over the region you want to select and then click to get a results list for the selected time-span. This enables you to identify why bursts of interest occurred in the blogosphere during the selected time. Another great feature is that you can include another search query in the graph and make quick comparisons between query results.

The outstanding feature of the results lists is the facility to read the posts in small preview windows. These are based on Blogscope's cached copies and they eliminate the need to click through to the actual blog. Previews of web pages have been used by a handful of web search engines, but never quite so elegantly as this. The reason why this can be done so well, of course, is that blog post texts are stable, readily available and easily handled by a search engine. The feature is so useful that it makes you wonder why every blog search engine doesn't use it.

IceRocket – excellent coverage of non-European blogs

Not only is IceRocket a blog search engine and an interesting trend tool, it also offers several other types of search, including some that are closely related to blog search. Among these are MySpace search, which lets you search in blogs and other web pages on Live Spaces; Twitter Search; and Big Buzz, which searches simultaneously in blogs, tweets, YouTube videos and Flickr images. You won't find a lot of information on the website about the search engine or who's behind it. In fact, if you want to contact IceRocket the only thing you can do is send an email from a contact page because there's no contact information either. This would ordinarily raise some suspicion, but IceRocket has been around for a couple of years now and is appreciated by many users for its excellent blog search engine. IceRocket is owned by Dallas-based billionaire Mark Cuban, who wanted a search engine that could tell him in real time how his new movie was being received by the public.

At IceRocket you'll find a search box and several tabs for selecting between Blogs or any of the other available indexes (Figure 6.8). Here you will also find a list of the Top Blog Posts that bloggers link to. Then there's a top list for movie

Figure 6.8 IceRocket offers several different search indexes to choose from

pages that bloggers have recently linked to in the Internet Movie Database; the top list of videos includes the hottest video clips in YouTube and Google Video, as measured by new links from blogs. The time frame for these top lists is 48 hours, but you can change it to 24 hours when you navigate to the expanded lists. Two other popularity lists, that aren't shown on the home page, are for top sports stories and top celebrity news, both measured by new links to official sports sites and celebrity gossip sites.

The Trend Tool is much like those described for BlogPulse and Blogscope and can be used to generate trend graphs for up to five different search queries simultaneously. The graphs are nicely outlined, using different colours for the different queries. You also get some detailed statistics on the number of posts per day, total numbers of posts and averages (shown as percentages). The time-span for the graph can be set to one, two or three months backwards from today. IceRocket also offers a free blog statistics service that you can use on your own blog to measure, analyse and monitor visits. Additionally, there's an RSS builder tool that you can use to create RSS feeds for your own website.

The Advanced Search form can be accessed from the results page when you've entered your first query. It includes the same options that we recognize from other blog search engines: searching for all the words, any of the words or an exact phrase, and excluding keywords and phrases. Two very useful parameters that are also included are searching in blog post titles and in category tags in posts. You can also search for posts from a specified domain or for posts that link to specific web pages. Another good feature is searching for posts written by a specific author. You can also specify any date range for your search. Special syntax supported in the simple search box are the prefixes title:, author: and tag:, which you can use in combination if you want to.

The results pages are neatly designed and an easy-to-read label on the left shows the post date. Under the individual hits there's information on each blog's rank and the number of in-links or references to the post. Posts that include YouTube videos have previews from which you can click through to the video at YouTube. Within the results page you can filter your search by date ranges. Surprisingly, there are no options within the results page for sorting by either rank or relevance. On the other hand, you can filter the results by language, which is good, because you can't specify languages in the search form. IceRocket indexes content in some 20 languages and has excellent coverage of non-European languages, including Arabic, Chinese, Hebrew, Japanese, Korean, Persian and Vietnamese. It also indexes some other common languages in the blogosphere, such as Russian, Greek and Turkish. You can also save searches as RSS feeds and generate trend graphs from the results pages.

Blog directories

A great way to find interesting blogs is by browsing blog directories. There are many of these around and some of them are very big. They're normally divided into categories that can be browsed separately, and generally you can also search them using normal keywords. In the bigger blog directories this is far simpler than browsing because of the number of blogs listed.

The **Blogarama** directory lists over 163,000 blogs in 26 main categories and one level of sub-categories. The entries show which country the blog comes from and its rank, which is computed from user ratings and ingoing/outgoing traffic, among other things. The listings also carry short snippets as descriptions and star ratings from one to five. There are also top lists, such as the Most Popular list, which is derived from outgoing traffic from the Blogarama entries. The most Highly Rated list, on the other hand, is based on ratings from Blogarama users. The directory is easy to navigate, but another layer of sub-categories would be more practical.

Blogcatalog is a community for bloggers and has a huge directory offering something like 100,000 blog listings. There are 17 main categories and one layer of sub-categories, with listings ordered by a ranking system called Blog Stats. The directory has an individual page called Blog Detail for each blog listed. This provides a description of the blog, the author's name, country of origin, language, rating and the most recent posts. You can also read reviews and comments on the blog and there are links to a few related blogs in the directory. The Blogcatalog social community has various blogger groups and discussion forums, which are searchable. You'll also find very useful links to blogging tools such as platforms, widgets, resources and services for bloggers.

The **Blogflux** directory has more than 120,000 entries that are approved and some 40,000 awaiting approval. It has only one layer of categories, consisting of over 160 different topics. For each topic you can view the top sites according to rank. You can also navigate alphabetically or by popularity, using a tag cloud to the left of the screen. Blogs can also be browsed by countries and languages. Each blog listed has a page with site description, tags, categories, author, language, geographical location and the most recent posts. Like Blogcatalog, Blogflux offers a number of services for bloggers, such as visual themes for different blogging platforms, MapStats for tracking your blog visitors and tools for creating polls and quizzes.

The **Globe of Blogs**, which features more than 66,000 registered blogs, has been around since 2002. The interface is simple to navigate and provides several ways to browse blogs. There are 18 main topics, with one additional layer of sub-topics. Blogs can be browsed by titles and authors can be browsed by names and, curiously, by birthday! You can also navigate by blog geographical locations, using either larger regions or individual countries. The blogs' locations are indicated by country flags – state flags if in the US. The information about each blog consists of short snippets of site description, author's name and location. No special services are offered, nor, apparently, are ranking systems used.

The **Eatonweb Directory**, also known as the original blog directory, is still active after more than 10 years. As mentioned earlier, the emphasis is on listing mostly quality blogs and developing metrics for ranking them. In this directory you won't find blog descriptions extracted from the actual blogs. Instead, there are short reviews written by Eatonweb staff. Because of this, blog descriptions are much more interesting and informative than in other directories. You also get pointers to related blogs and are encouraged to enter tags for blogs on the review pages. Three kinds of metrics are used: strength, momentum and overall – which is a composite of the first two. The momentum metric is very useful and is designed to differentiate between blogs that are in a healthy state and those that aren't.

As indicated above, there are many more blog directories to choose from. One of them is the **Technorati Directory**, containing approximately 60,000 blog entries divided into nine main categories, five of which have sub-categories. Blog description pages in Technorati include information on Technorati Authority, recent posts and recent reactions from other bloggers, and show whether the blog is on any of the Top 100 lists. You can also submit reviews of blogs to the directory. Other international blog directories worth checking out are **Bloggeries, Blogexplosion, Best of the Web Blog Directory** and **Bloggernity**. Also deserving of mention are **Blogdir.co.uk**, which is the most important British blog directory, and **Blogolist**, which lists only blogs written in French.

Websites mentioned in this chapter

Blog search engines

Bloglines Search – http://bloglines.com/advsearch

BlogPulse – www.blogpulse.com

BlogScope – www.blogscope.net

Google Blog Search – http://blogsearch.google.com/blogsearch/advanced_blog_search

IceRocket Blogs – www.icerocket.com

Technorati – http://technorati.com

Twingly Blog Search – www.twingly.com/search

Blog directories

Best of the Web Blog Directory – http://blogs.botw.org

Blogarama – www.blogarama.com

Blogcatalog – www.blogcatalog.com/directory

BlogDir – http://blogdir.co.uk

Blogexplosion Blog Directory – www.blogexplosion.com/directory

Blogflux – http://dir.blogflux.com

Bloggeries – www.bloggeries.com

Bloggernity – www.bloggernity.com

Blogolist – http://blogolist.com

EatonWeb – http://portal.eatonweb.com

Globe of Blogs – www.globeofblogs.com

Technorati Directory – http://technorati.com/blogs/directory

Web-hosted blog publishing platforms

Blogger – www.blogger.com

LiveJournal – www.livejournal.com

TypePad – www.typepad.com

Windows Live Spaces – http://home.spaces.live.com

WordPress.com – http://wordpress.com

Blog publishing software

Movable Type – www.movabletype.org

WordPress – http://wordpress.org

About the blogosphere and censorship

Blogspot: More Spam Than Anything Else – http://blogoscoped.com/archive/2005-08-29-n40.html

Global Voices Online – http://globalvoicesonline.org

Rebecca McKinnon's RConversation – http://rconversation.blogs.com

Reporters Sans Fontières: Internet – http://en.rsf.org/internet.html

Technorati's *State of the Blogosphere* series – http://technorati.com/state-of-the-blogosphere

Archived websites in the Internet Archive
Early filter blogs

Cameron Barrett's CamWorld – http://web.archive.org/web/*/www.camworld.com

Dave Winer's Scripting News – http://web.archive.org/web/*/www.scripting.com

John Barger's Robot Wisdom – http://web.archive.org/web/*/www.robotwisdom.com

Justin Hall's Links from the Underground – http://web.archive.org/web/*/www.links.net

Peter Merholz's Peterme – http://web.archive.org/web/*/www.peterme.com

Michael Sippey's Filtered For Purity – http://web.archive.org/web/*/www.theobvious.com

Steve Bogart's News, Pointers and Commentary – http://web.archive.org/web/*/www.olin.wustl.edu/~bogart/

Discontinued blog search engines

Blogdex – http://web.archive.org/web/*/http://blogdex.net

Daypop – http://web.archive.org/web/*/www.daypop.com

Feedster – http://web.archive.org/web/*/www.feedster.com

Popdex – http://web.archive.org/web/*/www.popdex.com

7

The power of RSS

Abstract: The XML format known as RSS enables internet users to subscribe to 'feeds' of information from other websites. 'Enclosures' allow media files such as podcasts and video to be attached to a feed. RSS is widely used to receive information updates from news search sites and from blogs. All the major internet browsers have RSS reader capabilities. A more flexible option for managing subscriptions and reading feeds is to use a hosted RSS reader, such as Google Reader, Netvibes, Bloglines, My Yahoo!, Wikio, or a news aggregator such as FeedDemon, which provides more options for managing your subscriptions and news reading. RSS can be used to receive news updates that are based on your own custom searches. The major news search engines all support RSS feeds, as do many of the blog search engines. The chapter also provides a review of podcast search engines and directories.

Key words: feed readers, feed subscriptions, podcasts, RSS, Really Simple Syndication.

Introduction

Today many news sites and blogs publish their stories not only on normal web pages but also in so-called feed versions using RSS. In this chapter we explain how RSS or Really Simple Syndication works and how it has come to be a key internet technology. We describe how to subscribe to RSS feeds using web browsers, web-hosted readers and news aggregator programs. A detailed examination of some of the more popular feed readers, such as Google Reader, Netvibes, Bloglines, My Yahoo!, Wikio and FeedDemon, is followed by an introduction to creating custom RSS feeds based on search queries. The increasingly popular video and audio podcasts that are recent additions to the media landscape and have their roots in RSS technology have their own section at the end of the chapter.

A short history of RSS

RDF Site Summary or RSS was originally developed by Netscape for users of the My Netscape portal in 1999. The idea was that website owners would publish articles on their own sites and the titles of these articles would appear on the personal home pages of My Netscape users. The RSS format was based on XML and was intended to be the glue that facilitated this form of web syndication. The My Netscape project wasn't very successful, but RSS remained interesting to those who were working towards a standardized syndication format. It was at this point that well-known programmer and blogger Dave Winer took over the RSS specification and in 2000 he launched the modified 0.91 version which is still used by some feeds.

RSS as conceived by Netscape staff had several advanced features for defining metadata using the Resource Description Framework. Winer quickly did away with these, favouring simplicity as a means of spreading the format as widely as possible. Not everyone liked this and an alternative version, called RSS 1.0, appeared with the metadata facilities back in place. In this new branch of RSS the acronym was interpreted as Rich Site Summary.

It was Winer's approach, however, that became generally adopted. Here RSS is interpreted as Really Simple Syndication. Winer released two more versions (0.92 and 2.0), in which he developed the standard a little further, before transferring ownership of the specification to Harvard University in 2003. The fact that Dave Winer became involved had the result that he added support for the new standard to his blogging software products, such as Radio UserLand. Others followed, and soon nearly every blogging platform featured RSS feeds. Big media came just a little later. In November 2002 the New York Times started offering RSS feeds and in June 2003 BBC News hopped on the train.

One of the additions that Winer introduced to the specification was enclosures, which had been proposed earlier in a draft by Tristan Louis. This was an optional element that could be added to posts and contain links to files associated with the post. It became the technical foundation for podcasting, where links to sound files, such as MP3 files, were distributed as enclosures. An enclosure can have links to an arbitrary selection of file types and is now also used extensively for video files.

In addition to the different dialects of RSS, another syndication format has emerged, called Atom. Since its start in 2003 Atom has become quite widespread, chiefly because the immensely popular Blogger platform has adopted this format. It's very similar to the Winer versions of RSS and today most feed readers support both RSS and Atom formats, so it isn't a problem for end users. Since 2005 both of the leading browsers Microsoft Internet Explorer and Mozilla Firefox have adopted the little orange icon with the white radio waves to show links to RSS and Atom feeds.

What does RSS look like?

RSS is, as mentioned, an XML format and it has certain defined elements that can appear in channels and posts. In this context 'channel' means the feed itself. The following information is based on the RSS 2.0 specification. The required channel elements include the title of the channel, the link to the channel and a brief description. Other elements that are frequently used are the language in which the channel is written, the email address of the managing editor, a tiny image (usually called a favicon) that is associated with the channel and may be displayed with it, a category designation and the generator element indicating what software has been used to generate the feed.

Then we have the elements that go with the individual posts or 'items' – which is the term used in the RSS specification. Every item needs at least a title, a link and a description. The description can either be very short, consist of a truncated snippet or contain the full text of the blog post or article on the source website. Most bloggers include their full content in the feed, while feeds from professional news sites usually don't. The items normally have additional elements such as author, a link for comments, a publication time and one or more categories.

If the feed belongs to a podcast the items will also have the element called 'enclosure', containing an associated media object. Another important element is called 'guid' and is typically used for a permanent link to the item. As you can see, RSS 2.0 is, in fact, really simple syndication and is very easy for the programmers of publishing platforms to implement. It's also very straightforward for search engines to retrieve and index the XML. If a search engine indexes the feeds of blogs and news sites rather than the HTML versions, it's called a feed search engine.

What is OPML?

This acronym stands for Outline Processor Markup Language – a name that doesn't shed much light on what it's all about. It's really just an XML file containing an unordered list of items of some type. For us, the interesting thing about OPML is that in connection with RSS feeds it can be used for storing feed subscription data. OPML files are extremely practical because they enable you to export all your feed subscriptions to a small portable file. The file can then be imported by another feed reader program, automatically implementing all your subscriptions in the new reader environment. All feed readers worthy of the name should be able to import and export OPML files, and you should learn how to use them.

Choosing an RSS reader

To be able to take advantage of RSS feeds you need a program that can read, interpret and display the content that is stored in the RSS format. There are several types of RSS readers available, such as stand-alone news aggregator programs, web-hosted RSS readers, plug-ins for mail programs and RSS support embedded in browsers.

Web browsers as RSS readers

The easiest way to try out RSS is to use the embedded RSS reader capabilities in modern web browsers. Some have supported RSS for a long time, while others have taken their time to catch on to RSS. **Mozilla Firefox** was one of the first of the major web browsers to include feed reading, calling the subscribed feeds Live Bookmarks. This feature was available in Firefox 1.0 when it was launched in 2004. Live Bookmarks was quite an apt description, as they were handled in connection with the usual bookmarks, the difference being that they showed the titles of new posts rather than providing easy access to normal web pages. In current versions of Firefox the default option is to subscribe using Live Bookmarks, but you also have the option of subscribing via one of three web-hosted RSS readers: Google Reader, My Yahoo! or Bloglines. The Norwegian web browser **Opera** also added RSS support in 2004. Another early adopter of RSS was the **Safari** browser from Apple, which has supported RSS ever since the launch of version 2.0 in 2005.

Microsoft's web browser, **Internet Explorer** (IE), had no embedded support for RSS during the long period during which IE6 dominated desktops. Thus many users of the other major web browsers began to harness the power of RSS a couple of years before IE users started to do so. Numerous plug-ins for handling RSS feeds within IE6 were introduced during this time, and many users started out by using these for RSS subscriptions. It was not until the launch of Internet Explorer 7 in late 2006 that Microsoft finally added support for feed reading within the browser itself.

The RSS capability in the new browser turned out to be well designed and easy to use, but it was not until 2008 that IE7 began to supersede IE6 as the most common web browser on desktops around the world. All major browsers now provide easy subscription to RSS feeds by entering the address of a feed or clicking on a link leading to a feed. Another way to initiate a subscription is to click on the feed icon on the right of the address bar. This icon is displayed if the browser automatically detects the presence of a feed address on the current page.

Although this method of subscribing to RSS feeds involves the least effort on the part of the user, it does have severe limitations. The most important of these is the necessity to use a specific computer and a specific web browser on that computer to access your feeds – meaning that your feed subscriptions will be inaccessible from internet cafes or when you use a different computer. Most people who need to follow RSS feeds use different computers at work and at home. Of course, this will not be a problem for laptop users connected to wireless networks while travelling or staying away from home. Another limitation of this subscription method is that an embedded reader doesn't have nearly as many features as a web-hosted reader or stand-alone aggregator program.

Hosted RSS readers

A web-hosted feed reader provides the most flexibility for handling feed subscriptions. There are many of these around and some have been in operation for several years, developing their interfaces and adding new features. Using a hosted RSS reader you can access your feed data wherever you are, using any computer connected to the internet. Some of these readers are just one service among many being offered by a major company, while others are stand-alone web applications. On many websites you'll find little icons on which to click in order to subscribe to feed content with some of the web-hosted readers such as Google Reader, Bloglines or Netvibes.

The user interfaces of the web-hosted readers can vary significantly, some leaning towards a more graphically oriented look and feel while others have a more text-oriented environment. It pays to try out several different readers in order to find the one most suited to your needs and fancy. Changing from one reader to another is normally not a tiresome task, and most readers provide export facilities using OPML files – your OPML file can be imported into the new reader, so you don't need to manually re-enter your subscriptions. It doesn't hurt to occasionally take a backup of your subscriptions as an OPML file, to be on the safe side.

Google Reader

If you're a big Google fan, and most people are, you may want to try the Google Reader. Initially it was available only through Google Labs, but for some time it has been featured in the selection of services offered by the search engine giant. Currently it's accessible by clicking on the 'More' link in the row of links at the top of any of Google's pages. Gmail also has a link to Google Reader in the row of featured links, so there's no need for an extra click if you use Gmail as your email client. The same applies if you use Google Docs for editing documents, spreadsheets or presentations.

The Google Reader interface has a vertical pane on the left and a larger window on the right. In the left pane are two windows called Home and Explore and below them you'll find your feed subscriptions. When you click on a feed the individual posts appear in the large window on the right. Sometimes you'll see complete articles accompanied by pictures, other times you'll get only the links to the posts or articles at the source sites. It's also very common that you'll see just the beginning of texts and have to click through to the full text. Note the handy Google Reader search box, where you can search for keywords in all text in all of the posts that you have subscribed to. This search feature is one of the strongest arguments for choosing Google Reader as your preferred RSS reader.

To start a new subscription, click the icon at the top left and enter the feed URL. If you don't know the URL of a feed that you want to subscribe to you can use the box to enter a few search terms. Matching feeds will be displayed in the window on the right, along with descriptions, post frequencies and the number of Google Reader users that subscribe to them. An icon below each feed enables you to subscribe to it. If you want to have a look at the content first, which is advisable, click the link to the feed itself and check out some posts. When your subscriptions become so numerous as to begin cluttering your list we recommend that you start organizing your feeds into folders for different subjects.

Google Reader offers a couple of interesting things that you can do with individual posts. As in Gmail, you can add a star to a post to make it easily accessible by clicking the 'Starred items' link. If you're not sure whether you've finished with a post that you're reading and don't want to forget about it you can check the radio button 'Keep unread' – you may decide to award it a star later on! Some of us like to organize things for ourselves by using tags and Google Reader will let you add tags to individual posts.

If you want, you can also share an item with other Google Reader users by making it public so that others can find it. At the same time you can add a note to the item both for your own benefit and for that of people who follow your shared items. If you choose to share items you should enter a little information about yourself in your profile. Your shared items page can be made available to individual users or to user groups that you create. This makes Google Reader an excellent tool for use among colleagues or friends who share similar interests.

Immediately above your subscriptions is a section called Explore, which lists recommendations of other feeds that might be of interest to you. These are generated by comparing your subscriptions to the subscribed feeds of other users who seem to share your interests. The recommendations can provide valuable pointers to feeds with related content that can be great additions to your own subscription list. You can also use the 'Browse for stuff' link higher up the left pane to find bundles of feeds. These are sorted alphabetically into several hundred categories. Each bundle features between 4 and 10 feeds that are selected by Google staff. You can also create your own bundles and share them with your friends.

If you prefer to use your keyboard rather than moving the mouse all the time, check out the keyboard shortcuts that can be used within Google Reader. There are a host of really useful commands that enable you to navigate quite freely without reaching for the mouse. These should appeal especially to users who frequently use text-based editors like Vi or Emacs, and they can speed things up considerably. You'll find a list of 'Keyboard shortcuts' under the 'Reading Your Feeds' link in the Help section. All in all, Google Reader makes a strong case to be a first choice among web-hosted RSS readers. However, there are a few others that are equally strong and offer some features that you can't find in Google Reader ... at least, not yet.

Finally, let us point out one great feature that's related to matters we'll discuss later in this chapter. This is the ability of Google Reader to track keywords or search phrases within four different sources – Google Blog Search, Google News, Twitter Search and Ebay (Figure 7.1). Using this kind of tracking you'll get all the latest results for your search expressions in the services you choose. These search results feeds will appear as normal feeds in your Subscriptions window.

Figure 7.1 Google Reader can track keywords in several sources

One of the web-hosted feed readers that has been around the longest time is Bloglines. This service is in equal parts a blog search engine and a feed reader and remains a favourite in both capacities with many users. The Bloglines user interface is available in nine major languages, including the biggest European languages and Chinese and Japanese. Bloglines has a very good stripped-down reader interface, intended for use with mobile phones and other hand-held devices.

The search functions of the Bloglines search engine are integrated with the reader, which makes finding interesting feeds an easy task. You can also maintain a blog of your own within Bloglines if you want to. Additionally, it has a variety of add-on features, such as creating several email addresses connected to your account for various purposes – for example, subscribing to a mailing list and accessing it like a normal feed within the Bloglines reader.

The upper part of the pane on the left is used to manage subscriptions, your own blog, clippings and playlists. Each of these has a separate tab with links and options according to the activities assigned to that tab. The feed tab is, of course, the one you'll use the most and is where you can add new feeds. You'll discover, if you haven't already, that many

Bloglines

blogs and other sites carry little icons for easy subscription to their content using Bloglines. Some of your own subscriptions to new feeds will probably be accomplished in this way. Clicking the 'Add' link in Bloglines opens a secondary window in the main window on the right where you can enter feed addresses manually. This window also contains the Bloglines Quick Picks, which are suggestions compiled by Bloglines staff pointing to categorized premier content. There's also a list of the 50 most popular feeds that have been subscribed to during the past day.

As mentioned earlier, it makes sense to create different folders within the subscription tree so as to have things nicely sorted into feed groups. When you click the title of a folder all the posts within that group are listed chrono-logically in the reader window. This means that you can easily find all the most recent posts within the group without having to click on each feed individually to find the latest updates. A red exclamation mark next to the title of a feed indicates an error in retrieving posts – the feed address may have become obsolete and you need to check to see whether it has been changed.

Sometimes no posts will be shown in the main window unless you click 'Display', selecting either 'All items' or one of the other choices in the drop-down menu. Before doing so, take a look at the list of keyboard shortcuts that is displayed under this menu. They're not so numerous as in Google Reader, but there are shortcuts for all the most important actions for navigating the Bloglines interface.

In the window with the posts all the text and any images belonging to each post are displayed. If everything is included in the feed you won't have to visit the source website. Each post is accompanied by an email icon so that you can send the link to a friend (Figure 7.2). You can also make a clipping or send the post to your Bloglines blog.

Figure 7.2 Things to do with an individual blog post in Bloglines

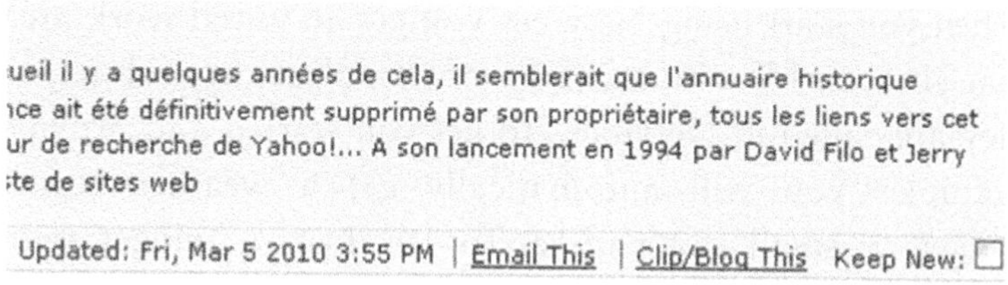

ueil il y a quelques années de cela, il semblerait que l'annuaire historique
ace ait été définitivement supprimé par son propriétaire, tous les liens vers cet
ur de recherche de Yahoo!... A son lancement en 1994 par David Filo et Jerry
ite de sites web

Updated: Fri, Mar 5 2010 3:55 PM | Email This | Clip/Blog This Keep New: ☐

These actions share the link called 'Clip/Blog This', which opens a window where you can choose the desired action. Clipped posts are accumulated and can be viewed later by clicking the Clippings tab. This is a great way to save stories that you want to return to and do something more with. If you choose to blog them you can also add comments and your friends can read your blog and learn about your discoveries.

The tab that we haven't discussed so far is Playlists – which isn't a place to keep a list of your favourite MP3 downloads. Here you can select feeds from your subscription tree and create a group of feeds that can be displayed simultaneously. In a Playlist, posts from different feeds are not mixed together, as they are when you click on a folder. In Playlists each feed is presented as a separate mini-window displaying the titles of the 10 most recent posts. This view closely resembles the default view of the Netvibes reader and certainly has its advantages. An interface of this type is also at the heart of Bloglines Beta, which is being developed as an alternative to Bloglines Classic.

Netvibes

One of the newer web-hosted readers, which has quickly gained in popularity, is Netvibes, from France. The interface is much more graphically oriented than in Google Reader or Bloglines, and Netvibes uses more modern web technology. When you start using Netvibes you get an initial work area that you can fill with a variety of modules – or widgets, as they are called in Netvibes. To get you started and provide examples you will automatically get a weather report widget, a small notepad, a To Do List, a widget with headlines from Google News and another with a set of thumbnail photos from a Flickr feed. Each widget is displayed as a mini-window on your screen.

By clicking 'Add content' you can browse the variety of widgets that you can choose from or you can start adding feeds. To find feeds, enter the address of a website and Netvibes will then provide you with a list of feeds available from that website. Of course, you can enter a feed address manually if you know the URL. Many websites carry bookmarklets for easy subscription to their feeds using Netvibes; you can also import your OPML file into Netvibes from another feed reader.

Your initial work area will soon be filled, so we recommend that you start adding new tabs with their own work areas right away. New feeds are displayed in mini-windows with the titles of the most recent posts; the windows are arranged vertically. You will soon learn to drag and drop the windows so as to arrange them according to your fancy. It's best not to add more feeds in the tabs than you can see without having to scroll downwards. This way, you can get a quick overview and easily scan through the post titles to find the interesting ones.

This is one of the greatest advantages of Netvibes – the simple fact that you can see so much so quickly. Both My Yahoo! and Bloglines have started to emulate the Netvibes interface. If you want to have many feeds in one tab and don't need to see all the post titles right away, just click the little arrow in the top left corner of the mini-window. This will collapse it into a horizontal bar. To expand it again, click on the same arrow. Netvibes will remember between sessions which of your mini-windows were open or closed.

Every mini-window can be customized and the whole interface can be altered graphically using themes and backgrounds of your choice. This can be lots of fun, but don't spend too much time on it. The main thing is that it should be easy to read and look good. By clicking on the 'Edit' link for a feed window you get a range of options from which you can choose the most appropriate look and feel for that particular feed (Figure 7.3). You can change the titles of windows, set how many posts to show, show timestamps, open items directly at the source sites and, if you want to, see more or fewer details for posts. There are also several window views to choose from, like slide-show, ticker, magazine and headline. You'll probably find the normal view the most useful after trying out all the others. The thing to remember is that it's possible to configure each window – and for some feeds the default options may not be the best.

Figure 7.3   **Each feed can be customized in Netvibes**

When you click on a post title a two-pane feed reader window is launched with the post titles on the left and the reading area on the right. Here you have access to more titles than you can see in the mini-windows. In the reading window each post has a link called 'Share', which allows you to email the post to a friend or share the post on your public Netvibes page, if you've created one. You can also share the post on Facebook or Twitter. If you're active in these social networks Netvibes can connect to them, provided that you supply your login information for these networks to the Netvibes application. When you've finished reading and sharing in your reader window you can close it and return to your work area in the active tab/mini-window.

Netvibes also has an intelligent way of handling podcast subscriptions. The mini-windows containing podcast feeds contain the titles of posts along with two little buttons. The first button is an arrow which you click to start a tiny embedded player that appears at the top of the page. The sound file will play until you stop it, and there's small slider for controlling the volume. You can see how long the streamed sound file has played and can pause at any time. You can also jump backwards and forwards by clicking in the horizontal bar that shows your progress within the stream. The second button looks like a miniature iPod Classic and clicking it enables you to download the whole file. This works best if you right-click on the iPod and choose 'Save link as'.

Netvibes introduced a new version of its feed reader in April 2010 with some new features. This version is called Wasabi and you can upgrade to it by simply clicking the 'Upgrade' link. Upgrading to newer Netvibes interfaces has never been mandatory, so if you're content with your current Netvibes version you can continue using it. However, you should know that Wasabi will update your lists of posts in real time, which is a big improvement.

Wasabi also introduces an alternative reader view that's similar to the default views in Google Reader and Bloglines Classic. To access it, click on 'Reader view' at the top of the page. To return to the normal Netvibes view just click 'Widgets view'. When you use Wasabi you can also have several so-called Dashboards. In the earlier versions of Netvibes there was just one Dashboard for managing your subscriptions using tabs. You can now add new Dashboards, each with its own collection of tabs.

My Yahoo! Reader

If you're a fan of the Yahoo! services such as My Yahoo! you can use its embedded feed reader. It doesn't have that many features but it does the job. When you first log in to My Yahoo! your Main Tab is active and filled with mini-windows or modules with a variety of content. Most of them rely on RSS feeds. You can delete unwanted windows from your Main Tab or create new tabs for your feed subscriptions. Unfortunately, there doesn't as yet seem to be any way to import OPML files into My Yahoo!. If you create a new tab you can add feeds by clicking 'Add content' and entering feed addresses. There are no tools for automatic feed discovery, so you'll have to find the addresses of the feeds you want to add.

The appearance of the My Yahoo! Reader is much like the Netvibes interface. You can change the background colour, try out different visual themes and fonts and rearrange the modules to your liking. By clicking More Options you'll be able to control a few other aspects of the reader. The default setting is that you see the 10 most recent post titles, with timestamps. Position the cursor over a post title to see a pop-up window with a text preview (Figure 7.4). If you click on the title you can read the post within the reader, without being transferred to the source site. If you want to get rid of timestamps and previews and be directed immediately to

Figure 7.4   Article previews in My Yahoo! Reader

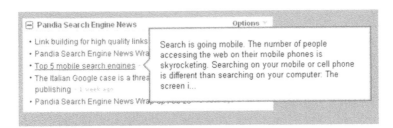

source sites you can change the default behaviour. The somewhat longer previews in My Yahoo! seem more user friendly compared to the shorter ones in Netvibes. Although you can see more details in Netvibes, they take up more space because they're displayed all the time, and not just when you hover the mouse pointer over post titles.

Wikio

The interesting French information portal Wikio has a news and blog search engine that tracks more than 200,000 media and blog sites. This is for English-language content, but it also has separate search engines for French, German, Spanish and Italian content. For some of these languages it indexes even more sites than are available in the English version. You can also use Wikio as a feed reader and for creating personal news pages, just as in other web-hosted readers.

Wikio is also a very active online community in which anyone can participate, and it's very common to share news pages and articles with friends. What's unique about Wikio is that it's also a web publishing platform, which means that you can publish articles you've written yourself on the Wikio portal. You can also comment on articles written by others. Voting on articles that you think are particularly interesting will increase their visibility in Wikio (Figure 7.5).

Figure 7.5 In Wikio you can vote on articles and share them in several ways

48 Hawaii-only species given endangered listing

Boston Globe (subscribe) | 6 hours ago

Honeycreeper birds, a fly and several ferns, trees and shrubs found only on among 48 species added Wednesday to the endangered species list, boost classifications by the Obama administration from two to 50.

0   add comment   ✉ send to a friend   f facebook   twitter   share

After registering with Wikio you can create your first personalized news page by clicking on the tab called New Page. There are two ways to get started. The first is to enter a feed URL in the box named 'Sources that you want to follow'. The second is to enter keywords that you want to monitor in the box called 'Your choices'. If you do the latter Wikio will track your keywords and show the latest matching results from its news and blog search engine. Whether you add multiple keyword searches or add several feeds to a page, the results will all be mixed together. This may appeal to some users, but Wikio doesn't currently allow you to read feeds separately. However, it does have links for exporting individual feeds and personal news pages to other readers such as Bloglines, Netvibes and Google Reader.

There are many other web-hosted alternatives to the readers we've covered here. **Pageflakes** from Germany is a good alternative to Netvibes, but you'll have to put up with some advertising in a window that can't be removed. The Canadian **MySyndikaat** is another great reader with powerful tools in a more text-oriented interface. You can do a lot of interesting filtering of the content with this reader but there are some limitations for free users. MySyndikaat calls the process of selecting and customizing content 'newsmastering' – a very good word to describe what one does with feed readers.

Using news aggregator software

The incentive for installing special software for your feed reading is that the better ones will have more advanced features than the web-hosted readers. The downside, of course, is that you'll have to install the aggregator software on the computer that you want to use for feed reading. There is a wide range of aggregator programs and you need to be aware that not all of them are all that good. Most news aggregators can be downloaded and used for free, so at least you'll probably not be paying anything. Wikipedia has a page of comparisons of feed readers where you can find good aggregators for platforms such as Windows, Apple and Linux. If you're already a Google Reader user and want to continue following the same subscriptions the news aggregator may be able to synchronize your reading with Google Reader.

FeedDemon

FeedDemon from Newsgator is an excellent choice to start with if you want to try out news aggregator software. We'll use it as an example to describe what this kind of program can do. It is proprietary Windows software but is free to use, and all you have to put up with is a little advertising window at the bottom left. NewsGator is also the company behind the popular **NetNewsWire** software for Macs and iPhones and **NewsGator Go!** for other mobile devices. FeedDemon can synchronize with your Google Reader account, enabling you to have several installations of FeedDemon while keeping them all in sync.

When you set up your installation you can choose to immediately import your subscriptions directly from web-hosted readers such as Bloglines and Google Reader, or you can supply an OPML file. FeedDemon has a powerful search engine for retrieving posts that match keywords you enter. It also offers many options for configuring the behaviour of individual subscriptions. If you like to follow podcasts, you should know that FeedDemon can also act as a podcatcher.

When adding a new feed you have the choice of supplying keywords rather than a feed address. If you want to do this, enter a keyword and click 'Next'; then click on the 'Find' button to get a list of feeds that have your keywords in their titles. Another great feature is that you can subscribe to a search feed, which is a feed of search results containing your keywords. Search results can be collected from Google Blog Search, Flickr, YouTube, Technorati and a few others. A search feed is different from and more powerful than the feature FeedDemon calls a 'watch'. This is because a watch only keeps track of posts from your subscribed feeds, whereas search feeds include results from all the feeds indexed by the chosen search engine. A watch can be a good choice if you have a set of feeds that you don't want to read regularly but do want to monitor to see whether posts matching your keywords appear.

FeedDemon has many ways of configuring the behaviour of feeds and feed groups. Right-click on a feed title in your subscriptions list to get a window in which you can edit the feed's properties. It's divided into four tabs called General, Updating, Advanced and Statistics. Under General you can choose whether to receive alerts when new posts arrive from this feed. You can also decide whether attention data (statistics on the number of entries in the feed that you click on) should be gathered during your reading of this particular feed.

You can apply filters from within the General Tab (Figure 7.6). Using filters, FeedDemon will mark all new posts as read or unread, depending on the inclusion or non-inclusion of keywords that you specify. You can decide where these keywords should appear, choosing any

Figure 7.6 Applying content filters in the news aggregator FeedDemon

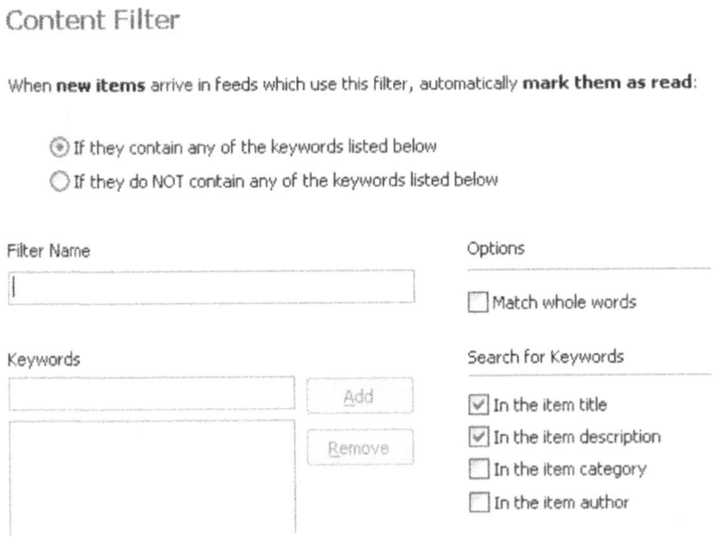

Content Filter

When **new items** arrive in feeds which use this filter, automatically **mark them as read**:

- ⊙ If they contain any of the keywords listed below
- ○ If they do NOT contain any of the keywords listed below

Filter Name

Options

☐ Match whole words

Keywords

Search for Keywords

Add

☑ In the item title
☑ In the item description
☐ In the item category
☐ In the item author

Remove

combination of item title, item text, item category or item author. You can create as many filters as you like. The FeedDemon filters allow you to do a lot of really interesting and useful things.

FeedDemon keeps the 200 most recent items of all feeds, but this can be configured under the Updating tab. Also under this tab you can specify how often FeedDemon should try to download new posts from the feed. Under the Advanced tab you can enable automatic download of enclosures if you want to use FeedDemon for podcasts. There are also options for ignoring anything older than a specified number of days and to exclude a feed from prefetching. The Prefetch option under the File drop-down menu is a convenient feature that enables you to download plenty of stories to keep you going when you have to go offline for a while.

The actions you can perform on individual posts are similar to those in web-hosted readers such as Google Reader and Bloglines, but there are a few extras. Posts can be starred, shared, tagged, emailed, marked as read or unread and even translated using Google Translate. You can choose between three views for posts – full, summary or titles only. If you have a large number of unread posts and start to feel stressed, why not use FeedDemon's panic button? This enables you to mark all posts older than a certain number of days as read. You can also use the Cleanup Wizard to weed things out in a more organized manner.

Under the View drop-down menu at the top of the screen FeedDemon has several reports that provide valuable information on the state of your feeds. The Dinosaur report will show you all feeds which haven't been updated for 60 days. The Feeds with Errors report lists feeds that return error messages, indicating that the feed is no longer available or has moved to a new address. These feeds can be deleted by clicking on the wastepaper basket icon. You should take advantage of these tools to prune your subscription list. The Attention Report shows which feeds you tend to read the most – it can be a good idea to sort these feeds together in a folder at the top of your tree for easy access.

RSS feeds – using pre-built and creating custom

Now that we've discussed the pros and cons of various feed readers it's time to focus a little more on the feeds themselves. Mostly, you'll be subscribing to feeds with content decided by others. This isn't your only option, because there are also ways to generate feeds based on your own input.

Websites offering feeds are mainly news and media sites, content management systems and publishing platforms, Web 2.0-based services, some search engines, some research databases and almost all blogs. It's up to you to find feeds with the right content. The feed readers have excellent feed discovery tools, and searching in blog search engines and directories can also yield good sources. Try searching for your favourite topic in Google News and Google Blog Search and look at some of the better stories you find. Do these sources have any RSS feeds?

News and blog search engines supporting results as feeds

One of the really interesting things about RSS feeds is that some services will let you create your own feeds adapted to your information needs. Librarians have worked for years with saved search strategies in expensive online databases that periodically generate lists of new matching results. Nowadays many library catalogues and research databases such as **Web of Science, Scopus** and **ScienceDirect** will let you subscribe to search queries as feeds. It's also possible to save a search expression as a feed in some of the news and blog search engines. The beauty of this is that it's all for free.

If properly set up, these search feeds will always display the latest stories matching your criteria. The crucial thing is to remember to avoid subscribing to a feed where the results are sorted by relevance rather than chronologically. Always sort the results of a search by date *before* you copy the feed address of the results list! (Figure 7.7) In other situations relevance will be the most desirable way to sort your search results, but never in this particular context.

Figure 7.7 Always sort your results by date before you look for the feed address. In Yahoo! News click on 'Time'

News search engines with feed results

So which search engines support RSS, and how do you find the feed address of the results list? Among the news search engines supporting RSS are the major ones such as **Google News, Yahoo! News** and **Bing News**. The results lists in each of these three are by default presented according to Relevance or Best Match and you will have to re-sort the results by Date (Google News), Time (Yahoo! News) or Most Recent (Bing News). Then and only then should you look for the feed versions of the search results.

All three of these news search engines use the familiar orange icon with the white radio waves. In Google News the feed can be found at the bottom left of the page. In Bing News it's under Resources in the left pane. In Yahoo! News it's displayed more prominently on the right, together with an icon that will let you subscribe to the feed using My Yahoo! Reader.

At the time of writing a search alliance between Microsoft and Yahoo! is taking place and it's not known whether this will lead to the disappearance of either of the news search engines or whether there will be a brand new one. According to what they have published on their mutual website, www. searchalliance.com, Microsoft will provide the search technology for Yahoo!, but while they say that it will include web, image and video search results, news search is not mentioned. Judging from the revamp of Yahoo! News in April 2010 it seems possible that Yahoo! will continue to run its own news search. Whatever happens, there will surely be support for search results as feeds in the news search of both companies.

Currently both Google and Yahoo! have Advanced Search forms in their news search, and these provide interesting options for the construction of queries for use in results feeds. The important thing to remember is that Google has separate searches for news in different languages. If you're content with English-language hits, this won't concern you. However, if these aren't enough, you'll have to set up separate feeds for different languages using the different Google News editions. Much easier, of course, is to use Yahoo! News, where you can select a set of languages that you want to search together.

When you use the Advanced Search form in Google News or Yahoo! News, take note of the possibility to limit your search to a specific news source. It means that you can generate RSS feeds for news sources that don't have their own RSS feeds, and in this way you can monitor any news source in Google's or Yahoo!'s index for mentions of your selected keywords. For instance, you can set up search feeds for the major press release services PR Newswire and Business Wire. In this connection you should also consider using the option to search for your keywords in the headlines of articles rather than anywhere in the article. This will help to focus your search when appropriate and will retrieve fewer articles – but hopefully more interesting ones.

Headline searching doesn't work so well for all searches, and you need to take into account the way in which news writers tend to use attention-grabbing but not always very descriptive headlines. You may have to experiment a bit to find what works best for your keywords. If you have a query that generates very few hits you should stay with 'anywhere in the article'. Remember that if your search query yields no hits at all for the time being, that's OK too. When someone does eventually write something that matches your search query you'll want to have a search feed active so that you know about it. Good choices for individual sources for feeds include major newspapers, news agencies, press release wires, scientific news wires and specialized news sources.

Before you enter the names of individual sources you need to check how they appear within the search engine and use the same format. For instance, if you want stories from the website of the British daily the *Guardian* in Yahoo! News, entering the word 'Guardian' as source name isn't enough. If you do so, you'll find many articles from the South African daily *Mail and Guardian* among your results. Instead you have to use the source name 'Guardian Unlimited' in Yahoo! News. In Google News, on the other hand, you have to enter 'The Guardian' to avoid getting articles from the *Mail and Guardian*.

Of course there are other news search engines with support for feed results besides the three we've mentioned here. **Wikio** has news search engines in five different languages and they all have feed results for searches. However, there are no advanced search forms and there will also be blog posts included in the results. **Topix** and **IceRocket News** are two other great news search engines that offer feed results. If you have trouble locating links to the feed versions in any of the mentioned news search engines, remember to look to the right of the address bar for a feed icon to click.

Blog search engines with feed results

It's very common for blog search engines to provide feed versions of search results and most of them have done so for a long time. Nearly all of the blog search engines that we covered in the Chapter 6 support this feature. So whether you use **Google Blog Search, Bloglines Search, Technorati, BlogPulse, IceRocket Blogs** or **Twingly** doesn't matter – you'll find feed versions of search results in all of them. Some of these are, by default, hybrids between news and blog search engines and you'll have to look for a way to separate the blog results from the news stories, if that is what you want.

Subscribing to podcasts

Podcasts have become increasingly popular during the last few years. The word 'podcasting' was invented by journalist Ben Hammersley, writing for the *Guardian* in 2004, and is a combination of iPod and broadcasting. You don't need an iPod to enjoy podcasts, of course – any MP3 player or computer with sound will do. Use of the word 'podcast' for a feed originally indicated that the format was audio. Today the term normally refers to both audio and video content. To start searching for podcasts that provide interesting listening or viewing you can try one of the categorized podcast directories.

Unfortunately, podcast directories tend to emerge, grow for a while and then suddenly disappear. One example is the excellent Yahoo! Podcasts Directory, which started out in a very ambitious way in late 2005 but lasted only two years. Some of the best ones currently available are **Podcast Alley**, **Podcastdirectory.com, Odeo.com** and the directory at **Podcasting News**. Many public and commercial broadcasting services such as the BBC, NPR, CNN, CBC (Canada), ZDF (Germany), Radio France, ABC News (US) and ABC News (Australia) offer a large amount of their programming as podcasts. There are also some newspapers, such as the *New York Times* and the *Guardian*, and periodicals such as *Time* magazine, *The New Yorker*, *Science* and *Nature* which produce quality podcasts.

To fully enjoy podcasts you should use a program that will automatically download the media files pointed to by the enclosure links in the podcast feeds. These programs are usually called podcatchers, and **iTunes** from Apple is currently the leading software for podcasts. If you don't want to install iTunes you can try using **FeedDemon** for podcasts, or use its bundled podcatcher, **FeedStation**. A comprehensive list of podcatchers for all platforms is maintained at **Podcasting News**. Take a look at it and try out a few before settling on what seem to do the work without interfering too much with your normal computing.

Podcast search engines

An exciting new development in the last few years has been the launch of a few podcast search engines that enable you to search the content of the enclosed media files. This kind of search is restricted to audio content – specifically, the spoken word. This doesn't mean that only audio files can be searched; on the contrary, much video material is being processed by these search engines. It's all accomplished by automatic speech recognition software, which creates transcripts of what's said in the files. The transcripts are then indexed by the search engine in the usual way. The accuracy of speech recognition is getting better and better, but of course there will still be many errors. It all boils down to how well people enunciate. However, this shouldn't bother you too much – the real point is the fact that there is a way to search this content at all.

Podscope was launched in early 2005. It was one of the best of these spoken-word search engines and offered feed results as well. Unfortunately, it seems to have been discontinued by its owners, TvEyes, in 2009. Another really good one was Everyzing, which was originally called Podzinger, also now, sadly, defunct. The in-line players implemented in Everyzing and Podscope were very well designed and enabled easy location and navigation of the passages where the search words were spoken (Figure 7.8). Podscope has been available again from time to time and if it's online when you read this you should try it out. It doesn't have snippets of transcribed passages with your search words in context, as Everyzing had, but is still fascinating.

Blinkx is probably your best choice at the moment, and indexes mostly video content. It boldly claims to have 35

Figure 7.8 The embedded player in Podscope with time indications for spoken keyword hits

million hours of video content that you can search. Blinkx uses a combination of techniques to index video content, speech recognition being just one of them. It supports feed results, which it calls SmartFeeds. Streamed video content can't be downloaded by a podcatcher, however, so you'll have to watch Blinkx in your browser. Most of the channels are newscasts rather than podcasts and Blinkx indexes hundreds of these sources. When searching you can specify that you want full direct-play content that can be played back in its entirety using Blinkx's embedded video player.

Websites mentioned in this chapter

Feed readers

Bloglines – www.bloglines.com

FeedDemon, NetNewsWire, NewsGator Go! – www.newsgator .com

Google Reader – www.google.com/reader

My Yahoo! – http://my.yahoo.com

MySyndikaat – http://mysyndicaat.com

Netvibes – www.netvibes.com

Pageflakes – www.pageflakes.com

Wikio – www.wikio.com

Podcast directories and search engines

Blinkx – www.blinkx.com

Odeo.com – http://odeo.com

Podcast Alley – www.podcastalley.com

PodcastDirectory.com – www.podcastdirectory.com

Podcasting News Directory – www.podcastingnews.com/forum/links.php

8

News discovery via social networking tools

Abstract: Social networking sites have become a major vehicle for news dissemination and comment. Microblogs such as Twitter have become very popular. This chapter reviews some of the search tools, syntax and directories that have been developed for microblog searching.

Key words: microblogs, news discovery, social media.

Introduction

As a result of the Web 2.0 explosion during the past decade, today a lot of the hot news and gossip can be found in or discovered through different social networking services and tools (SNSTs). Users of these tools spread news and information about current events by commenting on and frequently linking to news stories, blog posts and similar web pages. According to a survey published by Pew Internet in March 2010: '37% of Internet users have contributed to the creation of news, commented about it, or disseminated it via postings on social media sites like Facebook or Twitter.'[1] In this chapter we focus on some of the more important of these websites and on tools that we think will be of interest to people wanting to keep track of news and maybe also wanting to participate in commenting on and spreading news. Blogs are often called a social networking tool too, but because of their importance we've dedicated a separate chapter to blogs (see Chapter 6).

Microblogs

One of the most powerful tools for news discovery in social networks is the microblog. As the name suggests, microblogs are closely related to regular blogs, the main difference being the limited number of characters that are allowed in microblog posts. In the most popular microblog service, Twitter, the limit is 140 characters and replies are also limited to 140. In some other microblog platforms replies have no character limit at all.

A few years ago, before the Twitter phenomenon, Jaiku was a very popular microblog service. Jaiku was founded and developed in Finland and launched in July 2006. It was bought by Google in late 2007 and it wasn't long before the new owners abandoned the development of Jaiku. In March 2009 Google released Jaiku under an open source licence[2] and removed the important Lifestream function. This is probably why a lot of users moved to other microblog services such as Twitter. Some countries have their own popular microblog platforms, such as **Identi.ca** in Canada and **Bloggy** in Sweden, but Twitter is undoubtedly the current leader.

Twitter

Microblogs began as tools for telling your followers what you were up to during the day. The headline question when posting in the early days of Twitter, in 2006, was therefore: What are you doing? (Figure 8.1)

Figure 8.1 In 2006 Twitter was still intended to be used as a tool for telling people what you were doing

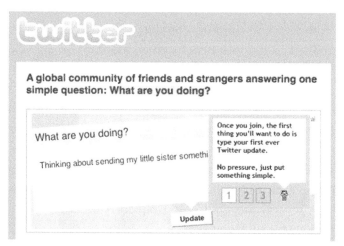

If you're using a Twitter 'badge' it's still the same question, but now without the question mark. Since Twitter has become more and more a news-related, or rather a current-events, tool the headline question has now been changed to: What's happening? (Figure 8.2) This is a good example of how Twitter has evolved in the hands of its users.

Figure 8.2 Today Twitter is mostly used to tell people what's happening and for linking to news stories or blog posts

Finding Twitter users

When you use a microblogging service it's possible to remain as a follower and explore content, trying to find valuable information, but you'll benefit much more if you participate by submitting microblog posts yourself. If you give, you will get. So register for an account in Twitter, start posting and become a follower of other people. In Twitter jargon users of the service can be called tweeple, tweeters or even twitterers. The act of posting is called tweeting, while the posts themselves are called tweets. If you are mutually following each other you're called tweeps. Unsurprisingly, there are several sites that keep frequently updated lists of all the neologisms of Twitterspeak.

When you first sign in to Twitter the question will arise: Who should I follow? Once you're logged in to Twitter a search option called 'Find people' is available. Using 'Find people' you can browse suggestions of Twitter users and find out whether your friends are on Twitter by connecting to Gmail, Yahoo! or AOL mail contacts. You can also use email to invite people to Twitter, and find people, organizations or companies you know that already have Twitter accounts.

Let's say you want to check whether the White House has a Twitter account. Search for 'White House' and you'll find the user account 'whitehouse'. There are two ways to check whether this is a real user or a fake one. If you know the person's website you can check there. Many individuals and organizations with Twitter accounts publish their Twitter stream on their website, in the same way as if they have a blog. In the case of the White House you won't find the Twitter stream on the website but there is a link to the Twitter account. The other way to check whether the user is authentic is to look for the blue seal indicating a Verified Account. Twitter launched the Verified Accounts service on

11 June 2009, but currently it's available only to famous or notable persons and public agencies.

Apart from the 'Find people' search that you can use while logged in to your Twitter account, you can also use the regular Twitter search at search.twitter.com. It has an Advanced Search form offering plenty of different search functions. If you search for a user such as the White House in the simple search box you'll get tweets that mention the White House. If a user's name consists of more than one word it's better to search the words together, as in 'whitehouse'. You will then get tweets where the user is mentioned as well as tweets from the user in question. If the user's name is a familiar word you'll also retrieve tweets that mention it in the text. Instead, you can search for the username with an at-sign, as in '@whitehouse'; you will then get tweets where the user is referenced, like in a retweet (to retweet is to forward a tweet in a tweet of your own because you think it's interesting in some way). If you use the search syntax 'from:whitehouse', however, your search will be restricted to tweets sent by this particular user.

Tweet search in Twitter

Unfortunately Twitter's search engine for tweets and tweeters in has its shortcomings. The real-time indexing doesn't always work perfectly, nor, at times, does the Advanced Search form. Using the Twitter search engine you can search for tweets in several different ways. Hashtags are a common way to tag or label a tweet, similar to keywords in databases. Using the hash character before the tag, like this: '#ipad', you'll get tweets about the iPad. Sometimes it's not easy to understand what the hashtag means. The website What The Hashtag is a wiki where some of the hashtags are explained. Many of them are actually abbreviations, as in this example: '#FSU'. According to What The Hashtag, this is an acronym for the 'former Soviet Union' and refers to countries in that region.

Many filters and limits can be applied within the Advanced Search form. You can also use Twitter's special syntax in a normal search box. The Advanced Search form has search boxes for implied Boolean operators (AND, OR, NOT), for phrases and for hashtags, and you can also restrict your search to 19 different languages. There are also sections in the Advanced Search for finding tweets based on People, Places, Dates and Attitudes. In the section called Other you can specify that you want the tweets to include links and retweets.

Using the special syntax, as mentioned earlier, you can find tweets from a tweeter, like this: 'from:stephenfry'; directed to a tweeter: 'to:stephenfry'; or referencing a person: '@stephenfry'. Geographical positions can be entered using operators like 'near:paris' and 'within:15mi'. Attitudes can be found using smileys: ':)' for positive and ':(' for negative. Finding questions is accomplished by entering a single question mark. Look at Twitter's page with all the available search operators to find even more syntax words. Of course, many users will find the Advanced Search form more convenient than using special syntax.

The world of Twitter applications

There are many other ways of searching or browsing for Twitter users besides Twitter search. Twitter has an API (application programming interface) that makes it easy to build tools using Twitter data, which is why there are so many tools related to Twitter. It's impossible to give a full overview of all the existing Twitter tools – but you'll find more than 1,600 listed in the Twitter application database, called Twitdom.

Tweepz for finding Tweeters

One of these applications is the Tweepz search engine, powered by the French search company Exalead, which is mostly recognized for its web search engine and enterprise search. Unlike some other search engines, Exalead has always tried to offer lots of advanced search options. Thus, Tweepz has several interesting search options for searching Twitter profiles. Tweepz currently crawls and indexes more than 15 million Twitter accounts.

If you want to search for journalists to follow, you can search in profiles like this: 'bio:journalist'. This will retrieve a list of all profiles mentioning the word journalist. You can then refine your search using 'bio:journalist bio:guardian' and retrieve both freelance and full-time journalists at the *Guardian*. If you change the search to only 'bio:guardian' you will get some irrelevant profiles, but on the other hand it will help you to find, for instance, a technology editor at the *Guardian* who didn't mention the word 'journalist' in his profile.

You can also use truncation and find results for a word stem, like this: 'bio:journalis*'. This will retrieve profiles with the words journalist, journalistic, journaliste and journalism (Figure 8.3). You can search for names and locations like

Figure 8.3	Tweepz offers a lot of advanced search options, like truncation and the NEAR operator

linux NEAR mac* loc:delhi   (Find!)

advanced search

Tweepz 1 - 2 of 2 for **linux NEAR mac* loc:delhi**   sort by: **relevancy** | # fc

Ravish (interactivecode)
I am an Entrepreneur, Developer, Designer, Internet Marketer, SEO & Linux Geek. I use Mac, drink coffee and love Drupal & Wordpress
Location: Gurgaon / Delhi
Web: http://www.shareminer.com

Sunny Kapoor (kapoorsunny)
I am a social tool. An Idea pooping machine, An entrepreneur, software developer, Practical Social media evangelist and A proud Linux user. I make things happen
Location: New Delhi [INDIA]
Web: http://sunnykapoor.tk

this: 'name:jean loc:paris', which will find people named Jean in Paris. Tweepz also permits you to use the proximity operator NEAR. This type of search operator is explained in Chapter 3. Searching for 'sweden NEAR norway' for example, will retrieve a profile with the text 'DJ/producer from Sweden. Based in Norway'.

Twingly microblog search engine

One of the best microblog search engines for searching microblogs other than just Twitter comes from Sweden and is called Twingly. It is well known for connecting articles in news sites with blog posts and for its excellent splog-free blog search engine. Twingly has similar search refinements to the Twitter search engines, but also searches SNSTs such as Jaiku, Identi.ca, Bleeper, Bloggy, Cirip, Koornk, Lareta, Linux Outlaws, Suffice to say, TWit Army and YouAre. The filtering options are similar to those in Twitter search, but not as many.

Directories of tweeters and similar services

There are many directories of Twitter users. One of particular interest is **Muck Rack**, where journalists working at selected news websites and who are active on Twitter are listed. These journalists are mostly located in the US and UK, working for news organizations such New York Times, the Guardian, ABC News, Fox News, the Financial Times, Wall Street Journal, Reuters and the BBC. There are currently 42 news sources in the directory. You can view the latest tweets and also get a list of top links that are currently tweeted by these journalists. At the top of the Muck Rack pages you will find links to similar directories of tweeters related to other professions or subjects, such as designers, musicians, coders, pets and travel.

There's a tool in **Google Labs** called Follow Finder where you can enter your Twitter user name or other user names and get suggestions of Twitter users to follow. In its own words, Follow Finder 'analyzes public social graph information (following and follower lists) on Twitter to find people you might want to follow'. In the first column of the hit list you get 'Tweeps you might like' and in the second column 'Tweeps with similar followers'.

The **Listorious** directory lets you find both individual tweeters and lists of the most-followed tweeters in different subjects. Other similar directories of Twitter users with many followers, organized by subjects, are **Wefollow, Just Tweet It** and **Twiplist**. On the websites **Twittervision, Geofollow** and **Tweetmondo** you can find Twitter users by geographical location. In **Twibs** you can find businesses active on Twitter, while in **Followfamous** you can find celebrities to follow, if you're so inclined.

Linking in microblogs

There are now a lot of services analysing links in microblog posts and other SNSTs. Very often microbloggers make short personal comments on articles or blog posts, frequently news related, and link to them. The links are nearly always shortened, using URL shortening services so as to leave as much space as possible for real words. Some examples of URL shortening services are to.ly, bit.ly, is.gd and tr.im. Every character that can be saved is valuable when microblogging!

Topsy – a search engine powered by tweets

Topsy is a search engine that analyses what people are linking to in Twitter. When you search in Topsy you'll get a list of tweets ranked by relevance. The relevance algorithm is based not just on how many tweets are linked to a web page; it also looks at how often the user linking to the web page has been retweeted. Twitter users who often get retweets can become Influential or Highly Influential within Twitter. English actor and author Stephen Fry is Highly Influential, according to Topsy, while Bryanrbeal, Senior Director of Cloud and SaaS Channel Sales at Savvis, is merely Influential. For most tweeters Topsy has no indication of possible influence.

The search options in Topsy aren't very impressive. You can search for words in tweets, but excluding words appears not to work properly. Searching with hashtags works fine, but using syntax like 'to:' or 'from:' with a username doesn't work. Topsy has a list of trending topics, and you can filter results by web pages, photos or just tweets.

Memetrackers and similar tools

Tweetmeme is a memetracker for tweets and gives you an overview of hot topics among tweeters (the term 'meme' refers to topics that rapidly engender much writing/commentary on the internet). By counting how many tweeters have tweeted a certain link, it shows the most current popular buzz on Twitter. Tweets are also categorized, and you can view a list of Top Tweeted Stories as well.

Convotrack is a bookmarklet that you integrate as a link in your web browser and is another tool that you can use to find out what has been said in social networks like Twitter about a certain article, news story or blog post. It can also be used to find what has been linked to in Twitter, FriendFeed, Blogs, Digg, Reddit or HackerNews. It's worth trying, because bookmarklets are often handy tools, just a click away in your browser bookmark field.

Another set of tools that is recommended for managing your social networks is the desktop clients for Twitter and sometimes for other SNSTs. **Tweetdeck** lets you update both Twitter, Facebook, MySpace and LinkedIn and is available for Windows, Mac and Linux. It also has versions for iPhone and iPad. The interface is impressive, fast and constantly improving, with new versions and new functions. Other similar desktop clients are **Seesmic** and **Twhirl**.

Digg and other social voting sites

In a social network site with a voting system a person can recommend an information item, for example a news article, to other users, who can then vote whether they think it's good or bad. Digg is undoubtedly the best-known website of this type. In Digg, users vote on stories that will, depending on the vote, move up or down in Digg. This is called digging or burying. The most Dugg (Digg jargon for past tense of Digg) stories are visible on the front page. There's an ongoing and intense debate about the value of this kind of voting site. Critics think it's too easy for users to game the system.

In June 2008 Digg introduced a recommendation engine that uses a Digg user's past digging activities to identify what it calls 'Diggers like you'. In this way it tries to suggest stories that different Digg users might like. Another website with a Digg-like voting system is **Sphinn**, which is focused on internet marketing and search engine optimization. **Designfloat** tries to do the same with design-related content.

Facebook for news and blog reading

When writing about social network services it's impossible not to acknowledge the power and influence of Facebook. According to Pew Internet, as of September 2009, 73 per cent of all adult profile owners now maintain a profile on Facebook, 48 per cent have a profile on MySpace and 14 per cent use LinkedIn.[3] Facebook is undoubtedly the leading SNST, and for many people Facebook is the most important entry point to the internet and a very important communication tool in its own right. Many experts believe Facebook is actually the main competitor to Google, and not Microsoft's Bing or any other traditional search engine. Because of the vast number of Facebook users we'll mention some possibilities within Facebook for monitoring news and blogs.

A number of applications have been written by different websites to make them available within Facebook. For example, you can read many blogs in Facebook. Go to the Facebook Application directory and search for a blog such as, for instance, TechCrunch and then add it. You can also visit a blog that you want to read and check whether it can be connected to Facebook. Use the same strategies as for news websites that you want to connect to. If you add the Guardian's Facebook application you'll be able to follow its news stories from within Facebook. The Guardian's Facebook application has different tabs where you can also follow its Twitter stream and YouTube channel.

If you want to connect to several blogs but don't want to read them separately (like a feed reader where you can mix several feeds) we recommend the Facebook application for NetworkedBlogs (Figure 8.4). Here you can add as many blogs as you like and all the posts will be sorted as a single list by date and time.

Figure 8.4 If your favourite blog has no Facebook application, try the Facebook application NetworkedBlogs, which allows you follow all your favourite blogs

There is a Facebook application for Google News, but apparently it hasn't worked for a long time. Yahoo! News, on the other hand, has a fully functional Facebook application that displays its latest news stories.

Google Buzz

Google Wave was predicted to be the new, trendy communication tool integrating real-time mail with chat, posting of links and photos. It was launched in 2009 but didn't become the success the developers were hoping for. In 2010 we've seen the launch of Google Buzz, which enables you to handle your social networking inside Gmail. You need to have a Gmail account in order to use Google Buzz, which integrates just below the link to your Inbox. With Google Buzz you can connect to your accounts in Twitter, YouTube, Flickr, Google Reader and Picasa. Your activity on those sites will create posts in your Google Buzz stream that can be shared with friends and others who want to follow you. Google Buzz has already become more popular than Google Wave, but only time will tell whether it will be a competitor to the dominant SNSTs.

Websites mentioned in this chapter

Microblogging services

Identi.ca – http://identi.ca

Jaiku – www.jaiku.com

Twitter – http://twitter.com

Microblog and Twitter search engines

Topsy – http://topsy.com

Tweepz – www.tweepz.com

Twingly Microblog Search – www.twingly.com/microblogsearch

Twitter Search – http://search.twitter.com

Directories and tools for finding tweeters

Follow Finder – http://followfinder.googlelabs.com

Followfamous – www.followfamous.com

Just Tweet It – http://justtweetit.com

Listorious – http://listorious.com

Muck Rack – http://muckrack.com

Tweetmondo – www.tweetmondo.com

Twibs – www.twibs.com

Twiplist – www.twiplist.com

Wefollow – http://wefollow.com

Memetrackers and similar tools

Convotrack – http://convotrack.com

TweetDeck – www.tweetdeck.com

Tweetmeme – http://tweetmeme.com

Other social networking sites, voting sites and websites

Digg – www.digg.com

Facebook – www.facebook.com

LinkedIn – www.linkedin.com

MySpace – www.myspace.com

Twitdom – www.twitdom.com

Notes

1. Kristen Purcell et al, 'Understanding the Participatory News Consumer', Pewinternet.org, 1 March 2010, http://pewinternet.org/Reports/2010/Online-News.aspx.

2. Jaikido Blog, 'JaikuEngine is now open source!', Jaikido. blogspot.com, 13 March 2009, http://jaikido.blogspot.com/2009/ 03/jaikuengine-is-now-open-source.html.

3. Amanda Lenhart et al, 'Social Media and Young Adults Part 3: Social Media', Pewinternet.org, 3 February 2010, http://pew internet.org/Reports/2010/Social-Media-and-Young-Adults/ Part-3/2-Adults-and-social-networks.aspx?r=1.

Concluding remarks

Abstract: This chapter presents key points from the text of the previous chapters. The remarks take the form of advice and recommendations and are not intended as a full summary.

Key words: news search.

In the process of writing this book we had to learn many new things, revisit our previous experiences and challenge some of our established views. This final chapter brings together some of the key points that we have discovered and that we want to highlight.

In writing about a topic that you're fairly well acquainted with you always run the risk of not investigating properly because you think you know already. However, news and blog searching is something that's evolving all the time, sometimes incrementally and sometimes in a great leap. The remarks and recommendations that follow are not presented in any strict order. They're intended to be advice of a practical nature, rather than a full summary of the book.

You should take advantage of the fact that many of the news search services that require you to pay for full text actually offer free searching. Use their search interfaces to find references to news articles and press releases, then try to find these on the free web, using the title of the article to perform a phrase search. Many articles from news agency writers are republished on several news websites. Some also find their way into article databases that are free. If you find the article in a web search engine and the live link doesn't work, try the cached copy.

Use the free news search engines that offer search results as RSS feeds to monitor searches for free. Remember always to sort the results list by date, with the most recent first, if relevancy is the default sorting method. Then grab the RSS feed address and add it as a subscription in the feed reader that you use. If you're interested in monitoring your search query in specific news sources you can use Google News or Yahoo! News. Go to the Advanced Search form and enter the name of your news source in the search box labelled Source. Occasionally you may have to make some trial searches in order to find out the source name.

Sometimes you want to search for press releases from a company that no longer exists or has been acquired by a larger company. If you've found interesting-looking references to releases you can try to find them for free in the Internet Archive. Use its Wayback Machine to find copies of the company's website that are as close as possible to the dates of the press releases. Go to the home page for a date soon after a press release was sent out, and look for a link that will give more information on the company, perhaps an 'About us' link. Many times there will be a list of recent press releases or an archive spanning several years. If you're lucky, you'll find the text this way.

Sometimes you will search a press release service, news agency website or other news source that doesn't offer its own keyword-based RSS results lists. In some cases it may not even offer pre-built RSS feeds for different topics. Go to Google News or Yahoo! News to see whether they index this service or website. If they do, use the Advanced Search form to do a search limited to this source. In this way you can monitor a source using a feed reader even if it doesn't offer RSS feeds itself.

In rare cases you may have references to news articles that you can't find even by using a professional search service. This is often the case when the articles in question have been written by freelance authors. In many countries the law forbids news article databases to provide electronic full text of stories written by freelancers. If the article has been published recently you may find a copy on the free web. If it's more than one month old and the source publication has a website with an archive, you may be able to find the article there. If it's too old you'll have to contact a library and find out whether the article is available on microfilm. If that particular library doesn't have the microfilm, it can probably order it from a larger library.

If you're using search alerts delivered by email, consider using a separate email account for them. Search alerts can soon start to clutter your inbox and this can become a problem. If you don't want to use a separate email account, see whether you can direct your alerts to a specific folder within your inbox. If your search query retrieves many hits per day you should probably go for one delivery a day. If there are more hits than the daily delivery can hold, you may want to review your search statement. Always try your searches manually for a couple of days before you use them as alerts, so as to find any problems with irrelevance. If you use Gmail, remember that it has an excellent search feature that will let you search through your email alerts quickly for secondary search words.

If you decide to use search alerting in the form of RSS feeds you should evaluate the pros and cons of the different types of feed readers. The easiest way to subscribe is to use the embedded feed reader capabilities of your web browser. When you click on an RSS feed link or icon the web browser will probably offer to subscribe right away. This may not be the best option, because then your subscriptions will be accessible using only that specific web browser on that particular computer. A much more flexible solution is to use a web-hosted feed reader, which will enable you to access your subscriptions from any computer with internet access. If you use your laptop everywhere you go, you can consider using dedicated news aggregator software. The best of these programs will provide an opportunity to use more advanced features, such as various filters that can be applied to your search feed results.

Learn how to use OPML files to store your feed subscriptions. This is a good way to make a backup of them so that you won't lose them if some problem occurs with your feed reader. If you export your subscriptions to an OPML file you can use the same file to import the subscriptions to another feed reader. This will enable you to try out several different feed reader environments in order to decide which is the most suitable for you. Even if you're very comfortable with what you have at the moment, a new feed reader may appear that offers a feature that you don't have in your current reader.

Perhaps you don't want to take the time to learn how to use a free news search engine such as Google News for free monitoring. If you're considering the option of paying to use a news or media monitoring service you should try to find out as much as possible about how it works before you sign up. Ask to see a list of source publications, websites and other services covered by the monitoring company. Particularly important is to ascertain how transparent the actual search process will be for you. Do you get to choose the keywords used and can operators be used within the search query? How are the results presented, and how often and by what means are they delivered? What determines the charge for using the service? Remember that if you have an account with a professional search service such as Factiva or

LexisNexis it will provide search monitoring as well and give you complete freedom to construct your own search expressions.

In some situations you may have problems with your search results because they generate a lot of irrelevant items in addition to the relevant ones. In such cases using negative search can be the solution. Look at the text of the articles that are irrelevant and try to find words that normally occur in these articles but not in the relevant ones. These words define the linguistic context of the irrelevant stuff and you can use the search interface to find out how to exclude them from the search. Sometimes you'll have to experiment a little to find the most effective choices. This way you will increase the proportion of relevant results – but you need to take care not to exclude words that might occur in the relevant items.

If you want to monitor the blogosphere you can set up keyword search alerts and RSS feeds using the blog search engines. When reading blogs you should always be aware of the number of spam blogs and fake blogs out there. Blogs present a great opportunity for people who want to manipulate readers. Especially in relation to product launches, you should be critical of overly positive or negative reviews found in blog posts or comments – it's an easy thing to create fake blog entries that boost the reputation of a product. In the same way, blogs and social media networks can be used to start smear campaigns and spread fake rumours concerning individuals. When you find a blog that comments on or writes about recent events in a way that raises your suspicion, try to find out as much as possible about it. If it was started about the same time as the event occurred this can be an indication that it's not to be trusted. It could actually have been created for the sole purpose of manipulating opinion in some way.

Free news search engines can have limited search capabilities, as can the internal search engines of news websites. In many cases a news search engine such as Google News can provide better indexing than does a website's internal search feature. Sometimes, however, it can be the reverse. There are several major news publications and broadcast news organizations that provide excellent internal search features, and they may offer more sophisticated search syntax and more precise indexing. Likewise, some of the news search services that offer free search but not free full text can at times give you better search facilities than the free news search engines.

One of the major problems with free news search engines is that they allow for very little precision. A typical situation is getting many irrelevant hits when you use two keywords, in which the words appear widely separated and in different contexts. When you use a professional search service this can be easily remedied by applying proximity operators. The most basic method for doing this is to specify how many words may appear between your search words. You may also be able to specify that the search words appear within the same sentence or paragraph. Tying your search words more closely together in this way will help you to get more relevant results.

If you decide to use a professional search service you should take time to read the help pages and try out different search features. There's little point in using a fee-based service if you search in the same manner in which you search in Google. If your search service allows you to search without cost, you should try out all the search functions so as to find which ones are most useful to you. Of course, this will vary depending on the search situation at hand. You will learn many new ways of searching that you had no idea even existed. With practice, you will gain a better understanding of when different search syntax is best applied and develop an intuition for what will work and what won't.

Another problem can be retrieving far too many hits, many of which are only marginally relevant. Sometimes you will need to focus your search so as to make sure that the articles that you get are mainly about the topic you're interested in. You can begin by taking advantage of the option to limit your search to headlines. This may not be enough, however, because headlines are normally selected to grab readers' attention rather than describe what the article is about. Therefore you should also try limiting to lead paragraphs. These will nearly always contain a few sentences that outline the contents of the text that follows. Most effective is to search in headlines and lead paragraphs together.

Free news search engines don't provide manual indexing of the text of news articles. This is where professional search services really shine. Several different indexing aspects may be provided, such as, for example, subject headings, industry codes, geographical regions and content types. These and others provide a way to add much more precision to your search, and they're especially useful when you have search words that are fairly common or have several meanings.

If you're interested in using Boolean and proximity operators together you need to learn how they behave when combined in search statements. A certain order of precedence will be at work, and you have to know it. Consult the help pages as often as you need to, and don't make any assumptions on the basis of what seems logical to you. Remember that you can manipulate the order of precedence by grouping parts of your search expression within parentheses. These can normally be nested to allow for additional flexibility and control.

Finally, we'd like to point out that there is a time when you should stop searching. This is when you have tried all possible search queries and search limitations and still can't find what you're looking for. In these cases it's better to start looking for a person, organization or company that may be able to provide the answers that you want. When you do, try sending an email or pick up your phone. One can never tell which will be the most effective and you may have to try both. Another possibility is to post a question in an active online forum, discussion group or mailing list that is dedicated to the topic you're interested in. Some of these forums may be searchable using a web search engine but many are not, and you may have to register first in order to be able to participate and read entries. Don't post any questions before you have thoroughly studied any frequently asked questions and searched the contents of the forum using the internal search engine.

It's difficult to foresee the future of news and blog searching because you never know when new search engines will appear that might make an impact by introducing novel solutions. If we look at the free news search engines, they provide excellent services and good search interfaces for the most recent news stories. However, you can never tell when a tool might change that you have come to like and depend on. Their developers have no paying customers that they have to think of, and they can come up with new ideas and discontinue existing components of their search without warning. These changes are not always for the better.

For instance, while we were writing this book one of our favourite news search engines suddenly dropped its Advanced Search form. In doing this it took away some of the most useful aspects of its news search – and it meant that we had to rewrite several sections. During the final stages of preparation of the book the Advanced Search form suddenly reappeared and we had to revise our text once again! This serves as a good illustration of the fact that the free search engines, while frequently providing good search facilities, can't be depended on in the same way as the professional, fee-based services. It all comes down to how serious you are about your news searching.

Further reading

Recommended websites

@-web Suchmaschinen Weblog – www.at-web.de/blog (in German)

Abondance – www.abondance.com (in French)

John Battelle's Searchblog – http://battellemedia.com

Pandia – www.pandia.com

ResearchBuzz – www.researchbuzz.org

ResourceShelf – www.resourceshelf.com

Search Engine Land – http://searchengineland.com

Search engine developers' blogs

Bing Search Blog – www.bing.com/community/blogs/search

Google News Blog – http://googlenewsblog.blogspot.com

Topix Web Log – http://blog.topix.com

Wikio Blog – http://blog.wikio.com (in French)

Yahoo! Search Blog – www.ysearchblog.com

Articles and books

Amman, Rudolf (2009), 'Jorn Barger, the Newspage network and the emergence of the weblog community', *Proceedings of the 20th ACM conference on Hypertext and Hypermedia, Torino, Italy, 2009*, p. 279.

Carlson, Matt (2007), 'Order versus access: News search engines and the challenge to traditional journalistic roles', *Media, Culture & Society*, Vol. 29, No. 6, p. 1014.

Chowdhury, Sudatta and Monica Landoni (2006), 'News aggregator services: User expectations and experience', *Online Information Review*, Vol. 30, No. 2, p. 100.

DiMattia, Susan S. (2007), 'How we teach (or should teach) online searching', *Online*, Vol. 31, No. 2, p. 34.

Elmer, Greg et al (2007), 'Election bloggers: Methods for determining political influence', *First Monday*, Vol. 12, No. 4, www.uic.edu/htbin/cgiwrap/bin/ojs/index.php/fm/article/view/1766/1646.

Glance, N.S., M. Hurst, and T. Tomokiyo (2004), 'BlogPulse: Automated trend discovery for weblogs', www.blogpulse.com/papers/www2004glance.pdf.

Halavais, Alexander (2009), *Search Engine Society*, Cambridge, UK: Polity Press.

Hammersley, Ben (2005), *Developing Feeds with RSS and Atom*, O'Reilly.

Kesmodel, David and Vauhini Vara (2005), 'A mixed blessing: News portals like Google News and Topix attract the masses, but irk some editors', Wall Street Journal Online 23 March, http://online.wsj.com/public/article/SB111151985359286597-hBb39gbCuTKJA1_hmsIeXHdB0gQ_20050422.html.

Murata, Tsuyoshi (2006), 'Towards the detection of breaking news from online web search keywords', *Proceedings of the 2006 IEEE/WIC/ACM International Conference on Web Intelligence International Intelligence Agent Technology Workshops*, p. 401.

Platakis, Manolis, Dimitrios Kotsakos and Dimitrios Gunopulos (2009), 'Searching for events in the blogosphere', *WWW 2009, 20–24 April 2009, Madrid, Spain*, p. 1225.

Rosenstein, Bruce (2001), 'Searching for news online and on the web: A head to head comparison', Online, July, www.infotoday.com/online/OL2001/rosenstein7_01.html.

Schlein, Alan M. (2004), *Find it online: The complete guide to online research*, 4th edn, Facts on Demand Press.

Sun, Aixin, Meishan Hu and Ee-Peng Lim (2008), 'Searching blogs and news: A study on popular queries', *SIGIR '08, 20–24 July, Singapore*, p. 729.

Thelwall, Mike and Laura Hasler (2007), 'Blog search engines', *Online Information Review*, Vol. 31, No. 4, p. 467.

Ulken, Eric (2005), 'Non-traditional sources cloud Google News results', Online Journalism Review, 19 May, www.ojr .org/ojr/stories/050519ulken/.

Index

Printed and bound by CPI Group (UK) Ltd, Croydon, CR0 4YY

03/10/2024

01040435-0009